Praise for Lewis Warsh's poetry

"What is at the core of the artistic work of Lewis Warsh? What drives his writing? To me, it is the courageous and exuberant interrogation of each existential moment and place and thought and action. He has been doing it his way through alertness, curiosity, beauty, stubbornness, perseverance and panache. In his output, there is an insistent drive for inter-cultural, historical, and personal inclusiveness. As he crosses paths with strangers, friends, family, students, lovers, enemies, admirers, he reminds us that writing is not only necessary, but a phenomenon that must always be in locomotion. The impact of Lewis Warsh will be felt for many years to come."

—Uche Nduka, *Harriet, The Poetry Foundation*

BLUE HEAVEN (1978)

"Lewis Warsh's poems are intimate & personal in tone. Somehow at the same time they are large in scale, like much of today's best work, & that they are highly ambitious perhaps has much to do with their scale. He makes use of the devices of the lyric, music, language, nuance, insinuation, plenty of surface, but his language is highly informed with intelligence (it is the pronouns for example who insinuate) and his music is white music, the music of the brain cells. Where the heart is just behind the words in their twists and turns through open and closed lines. Unlike his prose, which reveals everything, as it were, in order to state the mystery, his poems reveal nothing but imply everything. And his hands in your pockets, ah, warm."

—Ted Berrigan

THE CORSET (1986)

"*The Corset* is not a poem so much as a new way of seeing the world. In these sly and laconic epigrams, Lewis Warsh manages to explore the domain of sexuality with an almost perverse equilibrium. The facts are allowed to speak for themselves, and as the evidence mounts, we realize that we have been taken beyond the facts into the darkness of the human imagination. There is a stunning intelligence at work here, a fierce, deadpan wit that disturbs and enlightens in equal measure."

—Paul Auster

"Lewis Warsh has written an interesting poetic investigation of a strange custom of the Western world, mixing the surreal with the sensual to fashion a series of poems that provides an acute act of anthropological poiesis."

—Ed Sanders

AVENUE OF ESCAPE (1995)

"*Avenue of Escape* strikes me as a book of curious solitude—perhaps solitudes—the very territory where writing takes place. This is a 'progress of stories'—to adapt a famous phrase—from the child-writer to the writer-of-the-age-you-are. That the poem is not the world—that the poem is not the self—are clear foci, as if destiny were not inhabited, except by aphorisms and dispersed tales. It is a rending book, as if you had been torn out of it—words escape as from your 'starling's mouth.'"

—Robin Blaser

"In turn elegiac, discursive, ironic or deadpan, Lewis Warsh's poems trip the real while revealing the incontrovertible logic of his lyric. What's love got to do with it? Everything, for words and lovers are haunted by their absent objects in the same sublime way. Like a modern cross between Montaigne and Jabès, Warsh anatomizes this torment with the mastery and clarity of the possessed."

—Chris Tysh

"An anxious romantic enters night. An erotic muralist paints breasts on a mirror. A student of architecture unveils a 'new' New York in different seasons. A retired mechanic sees civilization sputter. All of these people are Lewis Warsh, incomparable scribe of late, late New York."

—Andrei Codrescu

TOUCH OF THE WHIP (2001)

"Poetry loves prose and makes brilliant babies with paragraphs and sentences. *Touch of the Whip* is a trans-genre pleasure, infinitely sage and sane. Warsh's narrative always speaks to itself from a lyric threshold. A postmodern Delmore Schwartz—yearning, mordant, suspenseful."

—Gloria Frym

"Lewis Warsh is at once psychological realist and idealist of love. This is writing from a life in all its mysterious richness."

—Gary Lenhart

THE ORIGIN OF THE WORLD (2001)

"The discrete (though hardly discreet) sentences in Lewis Warsh's new book actually merge to describe something like the origin of the world. As he says, 'Connect the dots to create a picture of something unimaginable.'"

—John Ashbery

"Given the complexity of this world and all the myriad people who are in it, these poems are poignantly articulate experiments, which reach out endlessly, day or night, so as to feel another is still there too. If one could ever doubt, Lewis Warsh proves again that the world exists, even after all is said and done."

—Robert Creeley

"It's incumbent on us to watch closely and observe well—to do otherwise is to miss what's happening. In this wonderful new book, Lewis Warsh sets out through a landscape swept with occurrence. As he looks about, somber image and glimpsed exegesis play off each other and the works unfold. Their lines flicker and figure; they resemble the light-images of which movies are made. They leap, fade, reappear—figuring out the world. As Lewis Warsh brilliantly reveals, this is the origin, always ongoing, of the world."

—Lyn Hejinian

INSEPARABLE (2008)

"Despite that Lewis Warsh is most closely associated with the community of writers who met at St. Mark's Church-in-the-Bowery from the late 60's through the 90's, his influence has been felt nationally and internationally. His work is rammed with life, deceptively casual, and psychologically acute. He can swerve from irony to Eros or from prose passages to precisely enjambed lyric with improvisatory slacker-dexterity. With his keenly urban eye, he's one of the terrific poets of New York."

—Forrest Gander

"'If you add one word to another,' Lewis Warsh writes, 'it's going to all make sense, eventually.' Much sense is made and pleasure given by a poet who has remained steady, melancholy, bemused and musical for many decades. I was especially moved by the poem about picking up the children from school. We are both ghost and matter now, everywhere we go."

—Fanny Howe

"Gently insistent rhythms and startling line breaks work in counterpoint through these poems, knocking the tender up against the harsh as they wind through their own labyrinth, constantly encountering the political quotidian shot through with memories, observations, and lyric detours. Always agile, always unexpected, Lewis Warsh's poems exemplify what good poetry must do—

wander from the prescribed path and find its own way through the newly-unrecognizable world."

—Cole Swensen

"Lewis Warsh stars as the hard-boiled detective on the trail of something ever-elusive but so distinct you can taste it (the words force themselves out of your own mouth). The camera careens woozily across the obliterated line of the grand narrative, as Warsh delivers breathless internal polyphonies with the bullet-speed of Bogart and Bacall, the balancing act of Buster Keaton, Thomas Bernhard's tell-it-like-it-is indictment and Sandra Bernhardt's audacious grace. These poems, crackling with phantom rhymes and rhythms hidden just below the sentence-surface, become more than poems, the way 'ideas are acts of love.' Warsh's imperatives ('tell me something you never told anyone') and admissions ('no one answerable except me') are such acts. He leads us confidently, and confidentially, in an unspoken agreement to feel as much as we can stand without breaking into pieces. 'Who can sleep?'"

—Matvei Yankelevich

ALIEN ABDUCTION (2015)

"Lewis Warsh is a poetry icon and a genius. His poems in *Alien Abduction* sing with a million inner and outer worlds that are both familiar and unfamiliar and speak of a new world of ideas and language that is timeless, gloriously happy and angry, and painstakingly beautiful. Warsh listens closely to everything, and in this book we find the mix of everything that makes up a life: Marx, Rousseau, sour milk, the songbook and the queen of hearts, mescaline, houses and bars and Paris. But in it too we find a life that is always strange because it is living and constantly changing and the eternal songs we must sing until the end of days and must thank Warsh for singing them first to us."

—Dorothea Lasky

"Nothing about Lewis Warsh's experiences is resolved, closed, or immune to his inner conflict. The reader follows him from an anecdotal phrase to a pan of the camera, from an often self-deprecatory meditation to droll truism, to astonishment at the obvious. He crafts his sequences so each relocation pertains, its simultaneity has purchase. *Alien Abduction* is as ambitious and successful as the best of his collections."

—John Godfrey

"'Rousseau said something about something.' We lean in closer. We want to hear what this very intelligent and charming person is saying. But, no dice. Not only will we never learn what Rousseau said, we won't even know which Rousseau the poet meant. But no matter. We are so seduced by this voice that we follow it down endless corridors, onto street corners, into flittings of the mind that remind us at each turn of our own, they seem so natural, so un-created. That's a trick Lewis Warsh plays, a sleight-of-hand, never more deftly than in his most recent collection, *Alien Abduction*. Prepare to be abducted. And to enjoy every second of it."

—Vincent Katz

OUT OF THE QUESTION

Out of the Question

Selected Poems (1963-2003)

Lewis Warsh

Station Hill

BARRYTOWN

Published by Station Hill of Barrytown, the publishing project of the Institute for Publishing Arts, Inc., 120 Station Hill Road, Barrytown, NY 12507, New York, a not-for-profit, tax-exempt organization [501(c)(3)].

Online catalogue: www.stationhill.org
e-mail: publishers@stationhill.org

 This publication is supported in part by grants from the New York State Council on the Arts, a state agency.

NYSCA

Design by Doormouse

Cover collage, "Untitled (1997)," by Lewis Warsh

Library of Congress Cataloging-in-Publication Data

Names: Warsh, Lewis, author.
Title: Out of the question : selected poems (1963-2003) / Lewis Warsh.
Description: Barrytown, NY : Station Hill of Barrytown, [2017]
Identifiers: LCCN 2017024765 | ISBN 9781581771640 (softfcover)
Classification: LCC PS3573.A782 A6 2017 | DDC 811/.54—dc23
LC record available at https://lccn.loc.gov/2017024765

Manufactured in the United States of America

CONTENTS

for Katt Lissard

TO THE READER

These poems were written on the Lower East Side of Manhattan; Bolinas, San Francisco and Stinson Beach, California; Cambridge, Worthington and Lenox, Massachusetts; Henniker, New Hampshire; and Brooklyn (Park Slope and Greenpoint).

The first poem in the book, "The Suicide Rates," was written in October 1963 when I was living with my parents in an apartment on the 17th floor of a building at 355 8th Avenue (just south of Penn Station). The window of my room faced 8th Avenue, and I could see the airplanes pass through the rotating beams of light coming from the top of the Empire State Building. I wrote the poem in one night.

The title sounds overly melodramatic, even for an 18-year-old, but I learned something in the course of writing the poem—how to talk about my life without saying anything directly, hinting and then going back over what I said in a different way. The poem was informed by my reading the poets of the San Francisco Renaissance who were my main influence in the early days along with the poets of the first-generation New York School.

"The Suicide Rates" was a first step in my education as a poet. The next poem in the book was written three years later, and there were hundreds of poems written in between that never saw the light of day. I think I catch something of the ambivalence—emotional, sexual—I was feeling at the time. I was in love with more than one person—how could that be?

The shorter poems sometimes sound like different people wrote them, and in a way that's true, and a good thing, though I recognize the writer in his various disguises no matter how many years have gone by. One criteria for including poems in the book was how closely I could still identify with the writer and what was going on in my life at the time. The most sudden shift, I think, happens in *Dreaming As One*, where the poems go from being dense and abstract to personal and direct almost without skipping a beat.

I kept going back to writing long poems divided into numbered sections so the last poem in the book looks like the first, but without

17

the insistent seriality and repetition of "The Suicide Rates." In "The Flea Market In Kiel" I was more interested in the adjacency of the different sections, not so much the hidden narrative, and each of the sections was written at a different time and arranged at an ineffable moment when everything felt right.

Arranging is sometimes more interesting than writing and often seems like the key to making something happen. The goal is to create an illusion of unity, but there are fissures where the connectedness disappears, and hopefully, if it works out, you can slip off into infinity at your own speed. This would be the ultimate goal of beginning and ending, and what happens in between—a whole life story.

Lewis Warsh
Manhattan, 2017

THE SUICIDE RATES

THE SUICIDE RATES

for Liam O'Gallagher

1

The bell was not a jar, when
I woke that night I was listening to the rain.
The wing of the gull was not hidden beneath the glass.

Lights, as they go on, watch
the shadows melt backwards
and the ladder cross the shade.
Like a drop parting with the brick, watch
this silence go unending.

The houses we occupy
are empty in our trust.

The bell was not meant to be rung
as an alarm. Small hotels and places
we can no longer assume vacant.

Small eyes blush at the windowsill
a geranium bends its wings into the crease, the
lights are the flashlights
finding the trail, breaking the line.

We can no longer assume
that the forest was only memory
                    The branches were like lead cables

Hands   palms down
personal ashes dead now

a calm fire in calm wood
encircles. I see a bluff

I see a corner of the mouth
a light breaking the line

Here
        I see a gambling room and the men
        stacking cards, I see

a bluff on their faces
the streaks of light go
the hint of light wavering

I see the child who is the hip breathing
and the bottom rise from under, undersea

The calm stack he took one number from his sleeve

2

How many ways to die for a window

It is dead night, far from home,
I sit back, dazed,
for a moment we affect the equality of places
of other nights, eyes, a casual stare, a price.

A longing that is not mutual
passes as a swan passes
other swans, a passing

The hunting lodge door fell open
the door of a gambling hall
was open, a jackknife

(he swam away)
the blade became a buckle, in
his belt there were twenty odd revolvers
how many ways to die was left unmentioned

We did not speak
thought my gesture made one/fifth
upon the bar
                          reveal itself

The child was not hard
he lived as long as a room is born
the left hand was not the first to go
it was the other, covering the deck

The doorman opened his door and a mouse
leaped out

3

The photographs that are dead before
the other photographs of his hands
were made public

Sperm or juice
and I am going to sleep tonight, early,
tilting the cup towards the blue uniformed stranger

Opening doors   feeling the board rock
as you dive

4

How long must we wait before these
numbers proportionally swell?
In a ratio at every fourth step
we take our chances

A board rocks a child refuses
to dive and dies

Lost in mid-afternoon
lost and the sun, pages
of sweat mount on my face

The grave is stone
the occupants of this room
turn obediently
Their backs are like lead
or so I would have it

A light does not turn with them.
An address book changes hands, how
many directions do we walk, walk
on our hands, on the joints
between our fingers, exploding
like underground mines miles away.

How many lines form at your door, are
they queues of longing, symbols
of that mid-afternoon
lost in sunlight, sweat,
crawling back across the sudden fine tear?

The job was not a bridge-builder.
It was to tabulate
the frenzy of the wall

to which you clung. Losing
sleep over the memories
you forget.

5

Rain can not
keep falling, it
releases
a tension.
        The bare back and arms of a cloud
move at my side. I lie, I
listen the sudden darkness of vehicles
down below. Sterility combs the helm.
My boat I will refurnish
for a casino on the sea.
All the gamblers in their tight black dress.

All the children taunting numerals
on my thigh. If there was not this fear
that the darkness throws overboard.

Lie awake, my own bare arm re
                            flexes.
They're gone tonight into the glamorous black beyond.
The gambling hall is closed,
a narrow line, a light, seems to move beneath the door.

In the realm of valises
I am all at once a passage
of tourists returning home for the weekend via my hands.
Of tourists replete with all their divine insights.

I lean, I lie awake, the
minute scratches embed your moving face.

At my elbow, a caution, a tension of springs.
The mattress   locked wire
makes sound the rain makes

I listen   I lose myself
I lose my hands
they are bound with the tossing
your plane is tossing in a clear blue sky,
it alights

6

Now I see photographs of the wild
and open vehicles of our time.
Too many means which transport the wavering eye.

A calm fire, fear enrages us, engraved
and partially naked, too many leaves release us.
Rain climbs down our skulls, the
pins of our forearms arc
                              in readiness, they
re-burst. These goods
we do not appraise. They
surround us with prices, the
numbers are on their tags. I seal
myself in.

Behind me a large window
and a party for small poems.
Small and gentle truces, watch
these keys clip wildly
hear them strike in the spirit
they unwillingly entice.

At most, the leaves do not
beg here to be swept.

From all sides, all lines
desert us and desire us.
From all windows this window
seems almost glamorous
to be alone. Write

these poems here
for the sake of writing,
at most it will make for us
an accumulative gesture,
a book for sonnet forms
and a grammar that leaves the ground.
                         Last night, in
a doorway on 53rd street, for
a moment I was holding
your cane, your homburg,
I was trying to explain myself,
a mania for my hands!
Last night on 53rd the
leaves did not
release, they
balanced. No
mention of your place
now, your presence
amid these poems, I
am writing to get
over, to turn
over

7

Almost blind light
and the hourly violence
of piano-keys
                    through whose wall this music comes

The victrola plays on, the
needle goes no farther than the surface
and breaks the thread

I sigh and see
my breath readily contagious

Almost blind
like light, yet
luminous, a rough shedding
shone on her ankle, countless
scratches on her fingers, her
fingertips a claw:
that is the wound, that
is, defeat. I brush
the back of her elbows

with my shoes, like
a lost detail
or the crows lost out at sea
or the crows amid other birds
pitting their wings on the insides of our voices
I see and seem to understand real stone.
It is comfort to brace
one's body on the real.
It is not enough
to keep this night from dying.

I see a bluff. I concede
all the dangers
and the comparable Autumn lights.
Somewhere the flash of a star
bleeds over his body.
A network of relative expressions
rapidly changes, changing face.

8

My own arm, my eyes.
The brick he lifts, was
it a mason
down below? In
the streets
we are given and we
accept, green
objects.

My eyes repeat that
the figures are
not discerned. They
are portions of the fire:
lost waking, blue moon rising.

Products of the calm.
A photograph that was his wrist
and the sleeve, the weightless flesh.

Quiet gambles it away.

9

Like small foreign villages whose gates have been
destroyed by bonfires
so the cities nearest my hands
are destroyed by the rust and the rustling of cool ashes.

Cool gray enters my throat.
It is painful to be foreign from you now,
to hear from others that your letters
spill like numbers
between the cracks of the avenues of the villages

that are not burning, that
have been spared

Huge windows corrupt me.
Between each ripple
the sun admits
duplicity. A
different face,
a room in which I lie and listen,
clawing for the grate
from which the gas breathes
in my hands.
                    It
hangs in space
above me
The loins hang

10

Small oaths snap like twigs
beneath our feet. Smaller
things impersonate
us, now that you are gone
a century of unappraised items
are released. The leaves

were not real gold,
they made replicas to establish
the dead end of the season.

Firm branches dip
against the blue arms
of the laborer, blue
lips from the cold
firm branches knead his flesh.

The leaves that the child touched
were almost real sounds.
Counting the attempts that the sun makes
as it emerges, counting the chimneys
and the smoke about to rise.
A dim light leads the way.
Through a crowd of countless deaths
your face emerges, a map
moving and charting the rain
across this glass.

Firm branches dip the blue, blue lips from the cold

1963

from DREAMING AS ONE

MOVING THROUGH AIR

A stone falls
and the expedient path
is blocked. We hide
in the bushes
because we are frightened of being attacked
from behind, from the boat
we are lifting our bows into the air
watching the arrows splash
taking aim, repeating the fire.

The wind on top of the gull streak, hindering
advances
we repeat   after an hour
you are immune
you see them die
like cubes of sugar in a tumbler
where you sit
the waiters, trays at hips, brush
through the aisles
you look at your watch and the angle of the tray
the growth of the long invigorating marrow
inside the rock
that vein you know now must be mined
you smoke and you look at the air and you wonder
about the water, the boat, the cooler
water under the pier,
you even enter the various waters
to test my judgement   yet
you are the only mind I ever desired
desire now out of habit
in the thread a fret sustains us, benches
under the trees
the beach, gum on the sandals, the net raised
because you cheat

THE CALIFORNIA POEM

The folds in a blanket are inseparable
from the flight,
and the heat in San Diego withers
like a sturdy branch facing
a bar outside customs
where we are taken
searching for forces from the outside
to control our lives.

But even as the bar
remains a palace for friends
to gather, a stranger
with printed cards
places our wallets on display,
and we return to know our own
signatures on the check
that has cancelled
in the hands of the
only cashier visible
behind the wire.

And California blinks
its moist brown eyes
in darkness
that reminds me continuously
how we are aging when we sleep
which keeps us up one
hour longer beside the set.

The sounds from your mouth intrigue me
as I'm asleep with you and birds
flying north to Los Angeles, San
Francisco and Seattle

                    press
their underfed talons into the flesh
drawing blood from us as sustenance
for they are powerless to sleep,
and age only as the overhead stars deny them darkness.

It is a rejoinder or excuse
for all the days in California,
and as flowers budge under
an expressway the streets
of soft clay grow disenchanted
with our steps
                    as friction
leads us away
from the principal highways
that we seek.

And headlights of new cars
might be flashlights
seeking our hands
as we search for the book
of travel poems left behind
in the car that has
stopped at the rest
for more gas mainly.

So evenings in San
Francisco say a
cell will be destroyed
by drugs
            and I wonder
if the bus will disappear in the night
and if progress remains commensurate
with our longing to find
the way

from this city to the next, and
whether planes carrying
dignitaries
really crashed
over Oakland.

Someday I think it will
be possible again, in snow,
to vanish
like electric wires carrying
messages to the west

as a day bed opens in a motel in Indiana
where a new and still different
road painstakingly
crosses the one we've taken.

The folds in the
blanket across
the sand bars in San
Diego and above our
heads the clouds

and the broadcast
beside our ears, filled
with white sand and pebbles
to determine the intensity
of light. And
must blood wash out
the memory of
those boys beside
the water as commandos
find their berths at
twilight amid the rocks

from which they see us
alone on a blanket,
facing the sea,

with the strength which
like trees impulsively trembling
                          preserves us now.

DREAMING OVER A PAGE

This field they've contracted
us to separate from its surroundings
I've stayed in bed watching as the
moon above it turns
its globes of earth with spit on every glacier
into landmarks hostile to language
spoken by tyrants
someone is looking over your shoulder as
you write in bed the window
holds a page of commentaries you guide
this pearl into the horizon then close your eyes

Simply filled with love their power
to be crass
you find yourself heading away from the park
down a path she is in the throes
of executing another assignment
the way it occurs and the publicity surrounding it
you think the glass burrows in
the sidewalk and are used
by the feelings that pass at great speed
a prude's entrance in the bar using
the language of the normal
spirit that the excellence of her modesty awards

Blocked by this person
we are heavier than grains locked
in a pearl stretched on rollers
tinting the sidewalk the laced boot
walks on scratching it out like the tip of a heel
among bruises from which you smile
the pathos culled remains linear
in its single-mindedness rebels and pushes

the curls aside
with the brute strength from her forehead
when she is too gentle not to adorn herself she
stares downward and the even cracks
of the restroom she prepares to enter

THE BLACK BOUNDARY

On the warm night
we approached the broken square sky,
where a railroad waited, and a town sped by
like a truck. Speed up
these labels of authenticity that intrude
through the blue as an elbow
crooks into the blackdown—rain
splashing the page, mocking breath, as
I appear.
The genius has spent the last years
of his life in attaining the freshness
and purpose of his young protégées—that's what's
admirable, to author a pledge
which breaks into pieces at his feet.
A heavily scented handkerchief wiping
the tears of her hand, the wind
stirring the folds of
the shower curtain
though no one's behind it.
Finally the two legs make contact under the desk
as pathos confirms the separation of two
friends—one in a dark suit
in the lobby of a deserted hotel
is staring at the sea through the rectangular
windows overhead. It is the sky
that makes the thought of death sickening,
and the eye, which when closed, resembles your flesh
pricked under a thimble.
Such patronage
coughs blood as we relax in bed,
flashing a screen of coil-springs to turn sideways,
to make room inside hollows of underhandedness
and bad taste. A note of instructions

on the long buffet which the guests managed
to view the possibility of eating though
most of them had decided to leave.
A continuous gurgling rose from
the bottom of the toilet, while behind him
on top of a brown hamper sat a pile of dirty
clothes—shirts, underpants, black
and red T-shirts and socks.
Brooding and malcontent, the night-time Angel
bit back. I feel
to be defied on all sides, at ease in it,
these smashed tubes, this dizziness
effaces and effects us all. Yet
I have been climbing elsewhere where
the question is candidly asked,
the questioner interviewed, the voice
cancelled—here I am
face   the movement
of a lift
into the rising light, covering nudity,
as crossing her legs
she turned, surveying our quarters—it was night
and the wheelchair had been left
in the garden, fenced in
amid black and bottomless tendrils
on a woody vine. Such emotions
recall the large painful ones I feel
every access of the rigid grooves
revealed, presence
I felt strongly on aimless walks
through late autumn and winter
streets of weapons
I let fall. For some day
you wake up knowing so little
is the sky of eternity is a white
corner combined with the sensual array

of passers
by the sidewalk where you will go.
When the lids close, free of death, a thought
of others seems to be yours,
incidents in touching detail cleverly
annotated out of sequence,
to come undone, to lift her
body into the air,
to pass the brick to a waiting hand below.
At dawn, we are the people who have begun
eating, preparing for work.
You advance towards
the cab in the sunshine
you have called back   a book kneels
on the skin of the meadow   to touch
sky (or better weep
to conquer itself   while writing   a
page   from the constituted reason
calls out   name my hands? anatomy
to teach   work is—to make an entry
else repeat   borrowed sleep
to work—while she says nothing)
That the choice is already made
for us with our breath
melting its shores

SONG

Our last night in Europe
You stayed in the hotel room
While I went out for a look
At what the prostitutes
Were doing in Amsterdam

A bus took me up to the gate
Down a footpath
It was remarkable
You were not beside me
It was a translation

In which all one's dreams
Have suddenly burst
In on the sleeper
But for enjoyment's sake
I slept I wanted to wake

Up bathed in the sweat
Of the girl who
Beckons from a doorway
Light her match
The threshold one's light matches

As one steps over it
To gather steam which trembles from a grate
And divide our last smoke
And after it's over
Take a walk along the quay

Which is a symbol of a long afternoon walk
I think it would be better if we didn't talk
And now I do not have to look back

On that room
Which enters my thoughts

And my heart wakes up from a recent stroke
Of fortune for I am alive
A prostitute stood smoking at the door to a cafe
She beckoned I went over
I stubbed my match on her throat

She collapsed I went inside
Her body it took twelve strokes
Before I collapsed
That was the first
And luck was with me: I went outside again

A sailor his uniform torn
Approached a window
Where a girl it doesn't matter what race
Displayed her goods
Behind the glass

She was looking at the sailor
Whose girl was waiting at home
For the day her sailor
Boyfriend would return
With the clap

As if a changed person had suddenly re-entered her life
That has come loose at the seams
A dress with nothing beneath it
Unzipped and hoisted over her head
So that her legs stick out

And the springs of the bed are bouncing
In the morning light
Which is steering a course against the window panes

Of her father's ranch house
Where they are living together in bliss

But that night so far off I could
Only translate it from knowledge
Of my own past
Struggled against the prospects of the moment
In the sailor's life

When the girl behind the window beckoned him inside
Actually she took the cross from around her neck
And bending lifted her dress
To the cross on her lips
As if she was going inside herself to be fucked

But I did not want to have intercourse with just anyone
In fact I only wanted to see what was going on
I thought of you it was our last night
Away from home
I did not do anything but walk the streets

Getting lost in my own thoughts
And soon I got lost I had taken
The wrong street
It was a dead end with a cross street
Our hotel was at the end

THE PACKARDS

The heretic's papers were spread out on the armchair

*

At the window, fruit of
spring,
you can bite again
against the weather

weapons I let fall outside
pharmacies, drowsy and bright

*

Air comes to the confused bends in the rail where
in a mirror lush food puts you
out for one night. Then it is the weather
at noon that prepares to spring on you
in December, a month ago,
blowing the lights out with a sob.

*

On long walks
a poorly tuned radio

in my world   my head
with a star attached
swims back

*

Useless—it was the wrong tree
but the flag in the school
breeze scans the men and women on my sleeve

*

A.... turned her head towards the open window
of the shop. The voice was low.
It did not sound like a man's voice.

*

Eighteen trees starting from the end
of the block
outside the pharmacy, with beards today
to the subway, station, steps

of a lamp post

"screen my heart"

*

Under the dog's neck
When the radio went on. Doctor
He moved his face away to
The pines, a deep thought.
The trees, for a few seconds they were
Real to him, his ears stopped
The river where no life could touch him.
He pressed his ear against the cold
Shrill whine. Dusty legs
Wondered why they had sent him
To this place, they feared the cobwebs
Were swaying on the unique bed.
Mown grass has the peppery smell

Of being crowded together on
This bed, and a feeling of dark apprehension
Came over him. I watch a horse
Gather speed, look at a movie
With you. Your words are the grime
On the side street, down towards the river,
Yellow in the cold glare of floodlights
In the yard. In the middle of the line
I repeated your instructions,
I puzzled what a stranger does to you
In a dream. Chunks
Of meat are marked
Cars following me as a thought follows
Us from the motel. Father
Has read these latinized titles
Aloud, but failed
And gave place to some smooth yellowish substance,
Checked by no one as he rubbed the sponge-
Like doll. It had some hair
But its legs did not tempt me,
The sponginess gave place to the tubes themselves.
Colleagues efficiently solve an aggressive
Blank to be expected as we sat at the breakfast
Table near the door. A tree blocked
Her hair spread and fell over the wheel.
But the living room shows its trimming of thick straw—
The bad mechanic sets the bread on the white cloth.

SECRET POEM

No one in the room
Nothing in the air
Light in the foyer
Girl in a chair

She moves her lips
At a rate of speed but
No one knows how fast
To her I am; she moves me

Gladly to innocently
Seek or receive. Go
My own way, hold
Her hollow hand as I can

LONG DISTANCE

A telephone
rings

in the country

in a phonebooth

in the middle of night

It's the operator
calling to ask me
for more money

I walk down the road, home,
alone into the night

I write this
poem in my head
as I walk

but when I get home
I forget it totally

WAYS OF SAYING GOODBYE

take it easy

        later

      see you later

              bye-bye

        so long

I think I'm going to split

"I hope we'll always be friends"

It was nice rapping with you; good luck.

DEFINITION OF GREAT

Momentarily

               the language of description is lost

      what you see with your eyes is enough, for you, anyway

but how to get the sense of what you saw across

                            to another person

it's possible

          through the spirit in your voice

       when you say

              "it was great!"

to convey

           what happened

              in that moment

    and it was great

             not only that

          it was terrific, and interesting too

                      it was nice

     and I had a good time doing it. I had fun.

You should have been there. Not only that, it was beautiful. It was inspiring.

SPLITTING

I am there.
I can imagine
myself.

I can do anything.

It is good to be clear.

Otherwise, I am thinking.

I can
be loving.

A future, next time around.

Next face.

Tired.

Separately.

There is
I was inspired to

I am not
who you
think.

Abuse, peace,
when someone asks, gives.

There was a reason

I came, went.

Asking's a pleasure.

My mind
changes constantly.

It doesn't hurt.

What was
no longer is

I can
go home.

Everything matters.

EASY DRONINGS

I'm more myself now than I was but less of me
is that self which goes out to you, still

inside that self there's a part of me that's
singing, it's not taking a tranquilizer (this

dosage may safely be increased as desired) nor
falling apart, collapsing on a rug at midnight

while the light from the Empire State Building takes over,
and reduces the assembly line of thoughts to "nothing."

Like my memory of the song "The Weight" which The Band
recorded in 1968 when all the children alive now weren't

even born, sitting in front of a fireplace nodding together,
easy droning in the clouds above our heads. If you go anywhere,

stay forever, because you can't go back to where you were, you
    can
for a visit, but you can't stay too long, and watch your past

spread out before you, like the inside of an eye closing, blinking
as you pull a sweater over your head, to block out everything

going down under the American sky.

FOR A MOMENT

Why doesn't the moment extend itself, I mean
the moment does, but you, changing through it, a
different person walks through the mirror, inside you
what is happening the day is beginning, you are
yourself, the parts of you everyone's seeing,
you are everyone you've ever been with for a moment.

WHAT I LEARNED THIS YEAR

typing doesn't disturb anyone

                                     Voices

    beautiful voices
singing songs

                             don't disturb anyone

footsteps
on a thin wood floor
               don't disturb anyone

    don't disturb me

please, don't disturb me

                           don't disturb anyone

              *

        This is what I learned this year

              *

    golden voices

                    sing beautiful songs

in your ear

               SHAKY   I learned

what shaky means
this year

but don't ask me

I learned that
there are no gurus this year, but I think I always knew that

learned what Scorpio means this year
but don't believe it

I've learned to believe in chronology
it's so supporting

I learned that everyone can take care of themselves this year

I learned a lot about silence

friendship

love
and flowers

I learned something about destiny this year but I've forgotten it
already

HOME

did I learn anything about home this year?

I learned that when
your heart said "Yes" you did it

and that when your body said "No"
you stopped

I learned that only love can break your heart

        but that your body can go on forever (so to speak)

I learned a little about energy, and distance

                I think I understand
            what "clairvoyance" means

I learned that people spoke metaphorically when they didn't want
    to hurt you

                    and how kind they were

I learned how people's lives connect

          and what separate means

        and the meaning of the word "useful"

              *

I saw myself turning into my father
        and I learned a lot from that

              *

I learned that other people's thoughts couldn't affect you

    and that it was a waste

        to think negatively about anything

I learned a little bit about ethics this year

I thought about Charles Olson

and Frank O'Hara a lot this year

I learned that I was hooked this year but I'm not sure to what

I learned what being self-involved means

I learned how to ride the music, all over again

*

this year

I borrowed the lives of my brothers

I saw where my demons came from

I learned to dig the blank spaces

I saw where not having money

could be limiting

in the most boring way

I looked at peace as more than a blurred possibility

as in "peace on earth"
or "peace of mind"

I learned that freedom's just another word

I learned that there was some other way

*

I learned what "learning to forget" means but realized I secretly
remember everything

I learned that unless you stop it just goes on forever

      that unless you stop it just goes on forever

           just goes on forever

I learned that no one disturbs anyone i.e. it's all in your head

      beautiful golden voices singing in your head

*

I learned what those lights blinking in the distance meant

      what the branch brushing against the window meant

      what the writing on the wall meant, if you took it seriously

         and the sense of "inventory"

I learned what it was like to feel fresh, almost virginal,
unembarrassed by it all

         and younger, even, than I was

INSIDE LONG TREKS

But is there an edge
inside the earth   acquitting
the rosy crimes with smoke
rolls over the ground   That in
innocence you allot
empty teeth shiver of emotions so strongly felt
on aimless walks   and the future
an old world slips away

The strip of leather has not reappeared
drifting from the blue motor
files, and the walls (with no south)
is why I do not wake like steel
at quitting time
follow   a mobile cut, the dull
humming prefers this

Father she blink a chair the mobile swings
and the walls fall away, fall like
a plane dive into a ditch   but
is there a ditch here   a blank
area between windows
south of this, forgotten, leaving
shoulders and walls exposed   humming while
he takes a walk to find records which tell him this

The walls he feels desperate to tell
someone this   in the spot begins my life
of emotions come back, on aimless walks
to record in innocence has touched and felt her
someone with him is cut down but the silence begins this

I leave my cigarette where I return
with a spot on it and the steel in my teeth
will not shiver. With shoulders exposed
at empty moments a cry with no future
bed   On walks to a strip records
the only person I look to

We eat everything, cough go blank
in a chair   cannot promise
aimless walks each in order to smooth
removes a hand   each time on walks
falls to shivering a cigarette is taken

down snow paths but he is cut down a mobile
appears   car I am inside her
my continued emotion prefers this

WORDS

Will I hitch
downtown to get
the morning mail, or
weep beside
the gas heater
which is whispering
DON'T MOAN, DON'T CRY
—words in the works
Bill, George and Larry
sent last Xmas, on the walls
like words in novels
spoken by characters
who aren't afraid to love me.
EVERYTHING IS GREAT, these words
on my lips, TERRIFIC
begin to sound like crickets
whose words work like music
turning on inside,
words which say what
you're feeling,
what you really mean,
THANKS for all your help and love,
words which go on being themselves,
JOY, PAIN, BEWILDERMENT
words erased by the mind
that goes on thinking them,
language, being made up of words
all different,
a letter from you filled
with words, all the same,
ending with
kisses   XXXXXXX
that are all the same.

INSIDE YOU

The point
at which you break off defining things,
listening, and experiencing, the waves
of your own voice, starting
to get it out through your chest,
which is inside you, as is your head,
with the hair on top brushed across the forehead,
stuttering which is not breathlessness,
you shrug knowing less of yourself and the
afterthought which goes on forever.

from BLUE HEAVEN

TODAY

Today's

  warm weather

surprised me, it's been

     so cold here

recently. The leaves stayed put

     there was

     no wind

and people

 on the bus across town

   looked

dazed. The

man at the door

            of the Henry Wadsworth Longfellow

 house

looked nervous

    as he took our money, and

   followed us around

from room to room. I tried to remember

                              what I knew

        of Longfellow, his poems

on my lips

        never seriously

as a child, and later

                              when we left the house

and walked across the street

to the Longfellow

        park

and sat in the little garden

in front of his tomb

I asked

        if you knew

        "Evangeline"

and you told me the story. Then we left, through

        a gate, down a street

which led to the river. After a short time we turned

up

        towards Brattle

and a dog

  barking in front

of a house

            leapt out at us

        as we passed.

      "Dumb dog!" I shouted, and walked on, home,

with postcards in my pocket

  of Longfellow

    his sons—Charles and Ernest—

      and his wife.

ON RUNNING

When running towards some distant point
But never sure exactly where, my feet pounding
In my brain, my side throbbing, my lung
A goal post holding up my eyelids, coming near
Dropping my last defense but still running and
Stopping to catch my breath,
    exposed
With my feet in my brain which is running without me
And my body which is trailing behind
Like running is supposed to mean faster
But no less wonderful than finally slowing down
Drawn like a magnet to the point I'm at anyway
Running and stopping at the same time and finally
And finally, not even out of breath, and not even running.

SOME TREES, SAN FRANCISCO, 1971

In the heart
A berry
Is hidden
In a plate of sand

One will leaf one's life all over again

Trackmarks across the same patch of land

The biker's colors
Crossing Haight Street

Darkness weighs lighter than a grain of sand

And one is glad
To wake up
On dry land

One will, won't one?
And then what?

Turn it over, and see
The patch of land. Quickly! before
The bulldozers tear up the land.
For a moment it seemed like it was getting
Out of hand, out of my hand.

DARLENE

Driving back from Berkeley today I start to go
through Richmond but miss the exit that says The
San Rafael Bridge not knowing it's the same as The
Richmond Bridge and finding myself on the way to
Sacramento decide to go back via S.F. but entering
the city miss the exit that says 'to Golden Gate
Bridge' and wind up riding down Fell St., then Fulton,
towards The Presidio; at the entrance, where I used
to hitch many times before, a young woman is waiting,
we make eye contact and before I turn she's in the
car, rapping about how she missed the Leon Russell
concert the night before and how the people she lives
with in Fairfax no longer like her but that all the
new people she meets like really love her, and she them,
and she's going to try to go to the concert tonight, but
first she has to go to Fairfax, and I hope you don't
mind me telling you all this, you're so patient, and
last night I met a really fine man but when I woke up
the $60 in my purse was gone, but it was worth it just
to get to know this man, and maybe I should go live on
a sailboat in Sausalito, I have a boyfriend, we've
been together 7 years but right now we're just not
getting along, and in my house the people I live with
whenever I cook anything like even before I eat it
they're on top me saying "Darlene—clean up that
mess."

FUNCTIONALISM

A fan blows through the hair of
The Good Samaritan and his face,
in its appearance among us, is as
good as gold. Do not persevere
a moment longer.
        Tiny arms, cleft
in chin, why do you upset the planes
from landing? Benched by
that same wind I put on my hairshirt.
I place a ducat in the hand of
a jester. I succumb to my chimeras.
I am the antithesis of The Good Samaritan.

IMMEDIATE SURROUNDING

I was just
walking home, anxious
to get some work done,
when I decided—out
of curiosity—to take
a different route, past
a building
facing Tompkins
Square Park I'd
lived in years ago, but
when I returned
home and sat
down at my desk the
phone rang, it was you
calling to say you were uptown, with
no money to get home and
could I come and meet you, "under
the marquee of The Winter Garden
Theatre" were your words, and I said,
"O.K....I'll be there," and went back
downstairs to
9th Street and First
where the car was parked.
The almost middle-aged Spanish ladies
who stand on the corner, near First, were gone
I guess it's too cold for them today, and
it's still a mystery to me what they do there,
in their tight clothes and makeup I thought
at first they were prostitutes but since I've
lived here I've never seen them proposition anyone, or
be propositioned in return (they're not very
attractive, actually, and if that is their vocation
I never feel they're totally involved, especially

compared to the young women on 12th Street near
3rd Avenue, who cruise outside The Dover Hotel, or
stand on the corner outside The Atlas Barber
School, you can't miss them) and
most of the time they're standing in the doorway
of the corner building or sitting on
crates in cheap brightly colored pants suits,
chatting obliviously among themselves.
The old Ukrainian woman who lives
on the floor below walks towards me
but pretends she doesn't see me
as we pass. A
man with a book leans
against the side of a blue
car and smokes. The Marxist-
Leninist Information
Center, a bookstore, is
closed. Two girls
in parochial school
uniforms, dresses with
purple stripes and white
blouses, are standing on the
front steps of a building
holding briefcases. (Earlier
today I went to buy the newspaper at
the luncheonette on the corner
of 10th and First, with the big
"say Pepsi, please" sign on
the door, and picked up a copy of The
Times from the stand out front, and
paid for it, but a few steps from
the store I noticed the headlines
were the same as yesterday's and when
I looked at the date
I read "Sunday" not "Monday"—it was
the first section of a Sunday Times, left

over—so I whirled
and went back to the store
where I shouted to the man, "I
don't want the Sunday paper," to
which he answered, "well, no one
asked you to take it," and
rather than arguing
I just gave him a hard look,
replaced the paper, took
a copy of The Post
from an adjacent stack,
and went my way,
my mind suddenly filled with
bad thoughts—imagine!—over
buying a newspaper.)
A big fruit market, "Three
Guys From Brooklyn," is open
all night, but the market on
the corner of 10th and First,
"The Night Owl Market," is closed,
and I hardly ever went there, not
even in my mind, when it was open
and I used to live in this neighborhood.
There's a building on the corner of 2nd and 10th
my father said is one of the oldest in New
York. It's big and red like the outside
of an armory.
An old lady with
white hair sits on the
steps of the building
opposite, every day, with her
cat lying stretched out on a window ledge
behind her. ("Don't touch
her, she's probably
full of diseases," I heard
one girl say to another, just

as she—the first girl—bent to
pet a cat that was standing, poised
to leap at the slightest threat, on the sidewalk
in front of the big white penthouse apartment building
on 9th Street and Third, and
hearing the girl's voice as I walked by, the voice
of the friend of the girl
who was befriending
the cat, it struck
me how the sounds people make
rarely match their physical appearances—as
in this case—women
who otherwise look
sensitive or intelligent, sounding
mindless and shrill, and men
who might resemble some definition
of handsome or goodlooking.) A girl
with a laundry bag swung over her
shoulder and a long dress
swirling out around her ankles
crosses the street
forcefully, like a woman
in The Middle Ages. This afternoon,
as I said before, I walked by a building
I'd lived in for 4 months
in 1964. The Swedenborg Bookstore,
open when I lived there, no longer exists,
and even the coffeehouse that replaced it
is gone. Two
men in raincoats and old-
fashioned wide-brimmed
hats trail behind me. A girl
and boy in their
teens talk to a policeman
in the lobby
of the P.A.L.

building on the corner
of 10th and Avenue A.
In the old
Peace Eye Bookstore,
facing the park, some
Polish men sit around
a table, playing cards.
I decide not to walk
through the park. On
9th Street two kids sit
on the curb watching their
father change a tire, a rack
of tires in front of
a storefront, and a sign in the window
—black lettering on cardboard—
"Flats Fixed."
I return home, looking
forward to the few hours
alone in the apartment, before
evening comes on
and the feeling and sense
of the air around me
changes, as my body
and everything I wanted to do
by day spills down a cliff
in my mind into night-time—and
before I know it I'm sitting
at the kitchen table, drinking
a glass of wine, while
the cat you found in Cambridge
and brought home, just
a kitten then, climbs
into my lap, and we—you and I—talk
about the possibility
of getting
it "fixed"

—"altered"
is the word the
doctor used
when we eventually
did it—though
the idea doesn't sit right in my
mind, completely, I try
to see into the future, his and ours, and
hope ultimately "the procedure" will be best
for him, and help appease the restlessness he must feel
cramped 24 hours a day in our apartment. Whatever,
coming home, the phone rings,
and with it my plans for working, however vague, disappear.
I drive uptown, along First Avenue, just
as the rush hour starts, then across 51st
Street to Broadway, and The Winter Garden Theater,
where you're waiting under the marquee, then without
getting out of the car
I continue down 7th Avenue, to 14th
Street, where I turn left and drive
East again. (It's easy, I've
learned, to drive and think
of things other than driving, but it's
too hard for me to really go off
into my own head. Last
year I drove almost
non-stop from Boston
to Atlanta, and for hours, towards the
end of the trip, I'd try
to keep myself awake—and I get
tired just remembering it—by thinking
or fantasizing every person I've been
involved with sexually, each
face or body flashing
briefly through my mind, and occasionally
I'd concentrate a moment too long

on the image of a particular person
and without realizing it
I'd be swerving off the road, or more often
an incredible 10 ton truck
would blow by me
and the rush of air
would draw me back into reality,
while the image in my mind and whatever
excitement I was feeling vanished.) Luckily, I find
a parking spot near the house, and as we
walk towards the entrance
I notice the super
of a building down the street, not ours,
stumble against a wooden crate, and kick it—
he's drunk. Our
only conversation
occurred the day
you and I moved
into the apartment and
unloading the furniture from the U-Haul-It
we'd driven down from Boston he
approached and said, "Hey, Amigo,"—which
surprised me, as he isn't Spanish (I guess
it was his way of saying 'I'm your
friend, you can trust me'), "Hey,
Amigo," (Hey, Brother), "do you need
any help?" and I said
"No….thanks," not quite convinced
of his intentions, though
since then
I've seen him working
with other people
on the block, and realize
despite his occasional binges
he's well known and respected
in the neighborhood; in fact,

without knowing him,
and without knowing why, I
like him a lot. ("The
one thing that
bothered me about the
church was the way, after
the ushers collected the money, they
brought it back up the aisle
and placed it on the altar
just after the priest had delivered
his sermon about the evils
of power and money. If
they're going to collect money
they should do it and split.
Who wants to pray to money?")
I walk into the kitchen and
light the stove beneath
the coffeepot. A roach is crawling
along the wall above the
sink. Dinner's
dishes are in the sink,
this morning's also, and I do a few
while waiting for the coffee to
boil. A
breeze through
the kitchen window
diffuses the food smells
with the smells of the kitchens
of all the other apartments whose
windows open into the
narrow courtyard between buildings,
and the music of the A.M. radio which the
woman who lives alone in the apartment next
door plays constantly whenever she's
home enters my brain
for a moment as I wash

off a dish and dry it then go
to the icebox for milk, turn down
the flame beneath the coffee,
and take my favorite cup
from the cupboard shelf, a green
and coral pink and white
ceramic cup which I
bought in Jap-
anesetown, San
Francisco, years ago
and whose existence, every time
I look at it, totally amazes me
not sentimentally necessarily
but as a reminder of past households
where I drank from it, and how possible
it is to preserve
and take with you
the parts of you
you feel most
strongly about, whether
they be your thoughts of
people or objects which by
accident or choice have
remained with you linking
your past and present, just like
the Egyptians did
when they died
and filled their tombs with
personal possessions,
or floated with them down the Nile in a barge.

STELLA MARINA

I make short shrift of feeling
Human, and guard my exertions for
Where they lead, a hundred humming motors
Pin me under, I acquit myself on steps
Before the populace and the sad-eyed judge
Anoints me with the priceless insignia
Of pride torn from a holy cup
By authorities so vested
They don't even show up for my trial.
Daybreak means something different
To noble Romeo, standing on a street
Corner with a beer in his hand,
A light in his eye like Leviathan
Rising from the smog, and a lot of hot air
Lifting the tie from his chest
In which he makes a covenant with the darts
Of light and pleasure, who attack from behind
Parked cars or step from doorways to make hand
Shadows on his forehead or like antelopes
Amble by comparing astrological signs.
The energy of the sun stored in the pores
Of the skin evaporates under the wind's well
Tempering influences, like harpsichord music
In an empty room, and 365 days later this happens
To the moon, and the shadow it casts
In relation to the light of the sun
And stars extends for miles along
The California coast, starting in La Jolla.
No first thoughts are preserved, only
The garbled sounds whispered in a friend's
Ear, and passed on to another friend, and so
On down the line, until the last
Person repeats what he or she heard

In a language as foreign as a bird's
And as high-pitched as the sonic boom used
To measure the ocean's depth.
But everything returns to earth—even
The peak of Mount Everest was once
At the bottom of the sea—and before
You know it you're inching your way
Through The Battery Tunnel, to where
The light at the end meets the abashed
Look of day, and the solstice rings its bell
In your ears, like a piercing shriek from
The top story of the World Trade Center.
This isn't the potion Romeo drank
As he sauntered towards his moment of
Destiny at the tomb, nor the embrace
That lasts a day, a few hours at best,
Then extends like the shadow of a blimp
Into a lifetime of speaking engagements
And boring $100 plate luncheons
Nor the luminescence which peaks in your
Eyes like flowers at noon then steals
Away to some backroom where the last
Cards are dealt out in a sequence resembling
The mating habits of the squid.

ARMED ESCORT

To circulate air (in a room) so as to freshen
Or drive out foul air, to give release to feelings
As in an outburst of profanity, to permit a passage
Of gas into the head and lungs,
    to examine
In public, bring out into the open, a grievance
Or problem, to oxygenate and the means to do this—
Any opening or device used to bring in fresh air—the
Lower chamber, as in the heart, or the cavities in the
Brain, used to pump air or blood from the auricles,
To receive blood and carry it
    into the arteries, where
Digestion takes place, where the feelings pass,
An air pipe or duct, the action of escaping, or the outlet—
The art of speaking so the voice comes from a source
    other than yourself,
Carrying on a conversation with a large puppet or dummy.

1000 POETRY READINGS

I'm going to begin with a series of poems, selections really, from
a book I began the winter before last around summer '73 actually
when I was staying with friends, friends of friends, in Seattle, the
series itself dividing into three sections so I'm just going to read
a few poems from each of the sections dealing with asceticism as
I see it and then try to bridge the sections…you know, bridges…
the last time I read having read the entire series but since then I've
written these other two parts, books really, so the second half of
the reading will connect with the first by some sort of suspension
or key with the continuity being that everything follows…please
smoke…alphabetically and chronologically as well, though in part
three, which I'll read last, with the quote by Wills, just something
I got off the TV really, and part of which was published recently
I hope you'll see how I've tried to tie everything together, with
life in Seattle which was really an exciting time for me connecting
with the other less exciting to me intellectually if nothing else
period in my life when I was working drudgery really like I'm
sure you know I'll try to end on an up note with my most recent
stuff which fits into the series or written on my last trip to New
York stands on its own as being central to the hideous grief I feel.

SONNET

If I turn into you
By force of habit, dint
Of luck, or just
Normally, as the occasion warrants
Not romantically, but because
Sifting through myself, I find
I'm thinking your thoughts, and you mine,
So it's possible both to inhabit
The body that sleeps beside you
And the concise fragments of the person
You thought you were, part in-
decision, part desire, part heavenly
Love, or all these things
Scattered over the earth, like sparks.

FALSE LABOR

First contractions
first snowy
night, I packed my
suitcase, started car

the baby dropped into
place, in my mind
a halo above his or her
face, I thought of people

I'd call or write to
with the news, no baby
yet in crib I leaned over, still
to stare into tightly shut eyes

of unseen sleepy baby, not yet

325 E. 10TH STREET

where I lived for 3 months, facing
Tompkins Square Park, in the winter
of '64, my first apartment, one
room really with a small dining area
and a tile bathroom
for $70 a month, $70
security and $70 paid to the realtor, D.D. Stein
to whose small office I made my way on a cold
March morning after poring over
the Unfurnished apartment columns
in the Voice, as if a voice
were speaking inside me, formidably
expressing everything I ever wanted to say,
formulating a plan by which my debut into the world
would be heralded by great bonfires of trash on every
street corner. Time to break the news to the folks,
"I'm leaving home," and call up Steve and Mike and
ask them to help me move
in Steve's VW bus, my books and records
and the bed my parents tell me begrudgingly I can take
along with the bureau, my old desk
plenty of towels and sheets, a pillow
and a jar of instant coffee, "just in case."
Along with a cup and saucer for the coffee, a pot
holder and a coffee pot, a hammer, some thumb-
tacks. Who knows what I might need, if anything,
except the feeling of feeling free, the
grimace of freedom shining down at me
like a shingle dripping raindrops onto the porch
this May morning.

WOOD FIRES IN FIELDS TO KEEP FRUIT TREES FROM FREEZING

A place I never
want to return to
inside myself, small and dark
like the detention ward
at Chico State or Sing Sing
as we cross the map over The Richmond Bridge and
    on into Sacramento
part of me spliced off and going in the opposite direction
another me fumbling in pants pocket
for money to pay man in tollbooth, Johnny
Mathis's brother someone
told me once
worked the tollbooth
of The Golden Gate Bridge

and I can hear Johnny Mathis all the way to Reno
singing "The Twelfth of Never" or the same song
set to Muzak in the local supermarket
where I drive up and deposit myself
as the soul flies out of the top of my head
and I become another person, older, antiquated, pursuing
tiny cans of baby food up aisles saturated
with pin curlers, women hidden
beneath them, and kids falling out of shopping carts
like jars of cider exploding
when you turn the lid. "I don't
forbid you to see him anymore but
don't kid yourself, if you continue
I'll leave—" a final
ultimatum lies on the sleeve
of the past, and words I spoke
in anger freeze the heart

till a voice in the heart, in heat,
expels them for good.

FOOTNOTE

If Lou-Salomé
had studied English
which maybe she did do
while Rilke
was learning Russian

she would have
known that 50 years
or so before
she was born
the poet Percy Shelley

newly wed
to Harriet Westbrook
(age 16)
and his Oxford chum Thomas Hogg
were living together

in a flat in York
in a "radical commune
of reformers." Like
a beam of light
on the collar

of history
the lump of organized
matter which enshrines my soul
informs me that the trivial domestic
labors which (in Shelley's eyes)

were merely time consuming
are the anguish and delight
of all domestic

relationship.
Washing a dish is a delicate

surgical
operation.
What I might have
done otherwise
I accomplished regardless, and with alacrity

the clean dish
my medallion
for time spent wisely.
The light of radium
in Madame Curie's eyes

was to no one's benefit
if despised by her children
like the plight of genius
disguised as a monster
whose children went insane

in the 20th Century
became a saint.
So there was no time to enter
into an innocent
ménage à trois.

Hogg's infatuation with
Harriet forced Shelley
to question
his ideas about
property

to rate friendship
above propriety
whose name was Elizabeth,
Harriet's sister,

as Nietzsche's sister,

Elizabeth,
whom Hitler
later visited,
made her presence
felt

when her brother Fred
and his friend Paul Rée
decided to
live together as
equals, in Germany,

with Lou-Salomé.

THE SECRET JOB

The Spring of '71
I was living alone
In San Francisco—broke
I went out and found a job

Embarrassed, I didn't want
My friends to know I worked, a
Snobbish impulse—the result
Of being alone and broke. No buffers—

My workday began at 8.
At 5 I boarded the bus
Home to my apartment
On The Panhandle. In between

I ate the lunch
I made for myself
Each morning, in a park
Opposite the library

A meagre meal
Among pigeons and drunks
For pigeons and drunks
If I told you you'd think.

It was a mystery, even
To me, what I was feeling
Except, being broke, I
Needed the money, didn't tell anyone

I'd found a job, what
Are friends for, anyway?
One morning, my boss, a Korean

Vet, took me aside
And advised me, not because
I wasn't doing my job
Properly, to quit—he was concerned
That, like him, I might make

This my life work, he was filled with regrets
After working 16 years, a young man himself
When he entered civilian life
With a wife and baby, he identified with me

Took the first job he found
And made it stick. I never
Told anyone I knew
About this job. I worked

Until I saved some money—
Then quit. Like an old friend
My boss sounded pleased, wished me luck.
"I found a better job," I lied

Over the phone. I sat at a desk
In my mind, holding on.
I'd had it—living alone. For money—
That was enough.

I didn't know what to think.
It was Spring in California
And I went to work, at a job
Any old person could do.

Drunk or alone or stupid—nothing fits.
What others might think—who cares about that?
"Why write your autobiography?
You're not famous!" I've heard that.

I made my lunch, and ate it
On a bench, in a park
Where the drunks slept
On the grass under the stars.

To feel embarrassed—everyone
Knows what that's like. It's better
To be poor, perhaps,
Penniless, than to feel that.

Who wants any ot it, I don't kow.
A secret life for a Scorpio—I've had enough.
I didn't want to do it all alone. An
Alarm woke me at 7. I ate breakfast, dressed.

One goes on properly, one lives among friends.
I could be anyone—getting
On and off that bus. People called
Me by my first name, at work—I had presence

My own desk, and a middle-
Aged man's concern.
He urged me to quit, and I did—
With his blessing.

from INFORMATION FROM THE SURFACE OF VENUS

DISSOLVES

Frightened of the dark, a dog barks in the night,
a child wakes and asks for a bottle of
juice but her parents are still sleeping.
The apartment was so small my parents slept on
a bed in the living room, I had to crawl
into the closet to use the phone which was
in the foyer or go down to the local drugstore
if I wanted my privacy (so-called). "Is
Allegra there?" I whispered. "She's not home, Lew,"
her father said. The booth filled with smoke
and the smoke filled my head as I shifted my weight
from one foot to another, lit a cigarette
and watched the local bookie swivel towards me
on a stool, a woman in a white apron
apply a sponge to the crumbs on the counter.
"Tuck me in," I called out in the middle of night,
and my mother swept in like an angel from the living room
to lift the covers and smooth them down around
my chin. It was dark; I had to pee, but I was frightened
of the short hallway with the two closets
(clothing and linen) leading to the bathroom,
so woke my sister and told her to "watch me"
while I went. Night, but not late, I walked
home from the drugstore, passed apartment buildings
draped in ivy and the cars on the parkway buzzing by.
Soon enough I'd be one of them, driving nowhere fast, alone,
at the wheel, with the window open, on a summer night.
I take a 12-ounce can of juice from the freezer, peel
off the lid and spoon the concentrate into a half-gallon
container, measure three cans of cold water into the container,
shake it up, fill my daughter's bottle with juice,
and go back to bed.

IN PUBLIC PLACES

European women hide
behind masks and fans
the composition of the
face is a mystery, like brevity
letters are disembodied messages
since the person writing isn't
there (as you read the message)—
what am I doing when you read
my letters?—Smoking off-duty (taking
a break) releases tension,
people on a break are different
than when they're working, act
different especially if there's
No Smoking on the job. Hide the way
you look (the composition
of the body) under clothing,
remember to maintain presentability
even if no one's there. Humming is a side
activity—you can be humming and still
thinking about something
else—same for chewing gum, smoking etc.
but during coffee break drinking coffee
is what you're doing
                        (the dominant activity)
"Haven't we met before?"
"Can I bum a smoke?"
Talk about something else other
than "work"—offering a cigarette
takes the weight off the main situation.
Whenever I eat alone in a restaurant
or even at home I like to read the newspaper
otherwise I look too hard at everything
and make myself, and the whole extant world

(everyone around me) unnecessarily self-conscious
eating, reading and eavesdropping too
("don't I know you?")
a failure to introduce, a failure to defer
pass a woman on the street late at night and proffer a word
to show you're not a would-be assailant, say
after making a transaction
in a shop in a foreign country
"Peace be with you"
then the cold-hearted Americans left the shop
brushing abruptly past the racks of saddlebags and daggers
while the smiling shopkeeper drank his coffee
ask a priest or a policeman or a nun, even, for directions
ask them the time of day
                              "do you have a light?"
change for a dollar
4 quarters   "the machine isn't working"
"sorry, I don't have any"

that guy didn't have any change
that nun thought you were going to murder her
that priest was on his way to catch a train
—who can blame him?

Orthodox Jews exchange greetings at a busstop
people in sports cars honk their blessings from Manchester to
     Liverpool
Americans in loud clothes visit exotic countries and fail to meet
2 complete strangers
                         ("scusa")
brush by each other on the street
a lady drops a handkerchief some men will talk to her
on a bus trip it's hard to sustain
conversation
                    ("I'm going to sleep")

if someone asks for charity suggest a charitable
organization to which the unfortunate
can apply
                              "I'm sorry, I have no money"
or ignore the person totally

talk about something innocuous as you ride up in an elevator
doors are boundaries whether they're open or closed
when the walls are thin problems of reticence get out of control
glances meet only to shoot away instantly

it would be rude at the end of a dinner party
to interrupt two people who have been conversing all evening
and introduce a new topic of conversation
birds on a fence stay a particular distance from one another
a bystander is likely to offer an apology
for imposing on the space of the couple
when a person allows himself to come into contact
with other people in a crowded place
the reactions
                         ("am I interrupting anything?")
can't be printed on this page

a general raising of voices
jams the opportunities of eavesdroppers
ambulances, police cars and fire engines
cut through public traffic
guests of a city may be given a motor escort
public kissing on the lips is considered an obscene act in Latin
      countries
in parks and beaches necking or arguing is tolerated
no one minds modulated light talk between two people walking
      together
people at an ocean pier can kiss each other deeply
for a suburban housewife meeting her husband's train
a light kiss is more in keeping

a church is not a social meeting place
husbands and wives go their own way
some establishments require dinner jackets
and keep a supply of ties handy
at summer resorts T-shirts can be worn in addition to swimming
    trunks
a young woman may slip off her shoes in public
an onlooker at a wedding procession may blow his nose discreetly

4/13/79

Use words to describe feelings?
I wouldn't if I were you.
Tracing back the history
of a symptom to its source, the
world of memory beckons and
we turn to it feeling
rude as the heart quickens
for fear some stranger
might intrude, some presence
like a court filled with jesters
and fools performing a masque
Ben Jonson might have written.
A point of light cuts an edge
in two. Where once there
was solitude now there's
an Ecumenical procession,
heads of people carrying babies and food
from St. Ann's to Trinity to the Church
on the Hill. Some people
are classified as "good"
by nature i.e. good people, while
others approach that state
after years of inner strife.
Think of buds struggling to burst
forth from the tips of branches,
or branches in which the buds
are imprisoned, encased in ice.
The cathartic method engages
our sense while resistance
fumes, head whittled
by an idiot out of a knot
of wood, the happiness that's
most apparent when it's

misunderstood, the surveyor's measurement
filed away for consistency under a full moon.
The comedy of thought animates the convictions
I know you knew, studying the classics
in a kind of take home test in self-
improvement, the amazing revelation
of a God you can see and who chooses you
to stand around and look observant, invisible
among those who know you and those who know
only the outline beneath the drapery like a
figure in a Renaissance painting, guarding the truth
or truth's symbol in the form of a chalice
or vase, that is what we do.
Odd that the air should feel odd
on Good Friday, exhaust
from too many cars surrounds
the steeple like a pod causing
static between bodies proportional
to the square of their roots, or
commodities becoming virtues which
exist to test our resistance
to speed or the whiskey
that made me clairvoyant
not virulent or virile
in the sense of having more
babies, let's get on
with our lives. As Milton
described "the parsimonious
emmet—in small room
large heart enclosed," so
the world consumes itself as
it multiplies, building walls
moats and turrets around
feeling mechanisms that were
inferior models to begin with.
Too comatose to know the difference

between what's secret
and what's real, I wake from a bad dream
and fire off a leaf to the master
whose name is plastered to the window
like an astringent. Lights
in the houses along Cliffwood
go out for the night, the
people we know by sight
turning over beneath the blinds.
The immediacy of the message
is lost in the history of a daily
life, kindled in privacy
and sparked by a belief
in what lies beyond: the
UPS man who arrived
at the wrong door and became
a fixture. A pipe on the grass,
different makes and models and brand
names attributed to gods and goddesses,
the anecdote splashing around in a pool
of associations back to who knows when,
following the thread beneath the door.
Who would take innocence to be more
than a reflection, an attitude towards night
as lightning approaches on waves of sound but
misses the point where even thought
could do no damage,
rummaging around like a pen
poised mid-air above a pad.
Body, restless as a flag, condition
some normal beauty to define
these eyes so hollow and sad,
linger longer than the weird
taste, or testament, of the past
which recreates itself as a series
of integers in the shape of dowagers

walking through a town square with
buckets of water balanced on their
heads: it's laundry day, the
shabby housecoats blowing across
cobblestones, impermanent
beauty raised to the highest
power, at peace again.

NINE HYMNS

1

Enigmas of feeling get lost
In the stream, and a shoe
Loses its companion like a hand
In marriage, but one shoe
Will not do, today, needs a brother or sister
For incestuous carnage is part
Of the New England tradition

There's a filling station I should stop
At on the side of the road

And the other shoe fits   as life, with all its tendencies
Feminine and masculine, creates a hierarchy
In order to develop and sustain its identity
By entering the landscape, thinking himself back into the picture
Or her, with her, its cardinal function is a fantasy
The observation of the self brings him in touch with reality
Not the thin line of sentiment between sanity
And going mad
                but the object
Of other people's feelings
Revealing the body's
Needs, in absentia.

2

The cars that pass going in the opposite direction
blind you momentarily, then they dim their brights
as a signal to you that they're fully conscious
and awake drivers not drunk teenagers, driving by night

the orchestra of solitude has assembled for your pleasure
whole families with kids curled asleep on someone's lap
the cars that were once behind you are passing on the right
a knife twisted through the lines of the purest impression

going home takes time, it's been a long day
one leg follows the other—would you like some tea?
first impressions leave lasting depressions
you give them your money and they hand you a key

in the motel there's a desk where I'll sit and compress
the thoughts in my head till they turn to dust
like rust at the bottom of an old canteen
and write a letter to the person I trust

the pleasures of the day, though uneventful, lead to the point
    where one can say
I came this far, like a child in your arms
two aspirin   a bath   a cup of tea
tomorrow I'll go see the crocodiles in the park

send you a postcard from the land of the free

3

Words left unspoken on a summer morning
when the colors of the light could be mistaken
for thunder, the act of love
mistaken for murder as the act of life and birth
is like life itself, that thought dispensed
in the Biblical sense when a voice answers
and it isn't you
but a portrait in the form of a composite
that leaves neither promises
nor regrets, turns on a phrase
about the weather or turns over in bed.

Feelings that have an extemporaneous way
of appearing on the surface without regard
for what lies beneath or how their meanings
might be misconstrued by someone you don't know
as well as others who had listened and not even heard
what you were saying, despite great pains
to spell it out in terms someone who couldn't
care less would acknowledge. A sign
in a window reads "Newspapers sold here"
but it wasn't the news of the world
I wanted, reduced to tears at the scale
and the immensity of the drama, but the hope
that the effortless gathering together
of everything I'd seen or done or read
would join with my imagination to kindle the experiences
of others, as if all the air to breathe
were riding the waves in our direction,
consecrating a space for the joy of hearing it said.

4

Looking at me from above
is it your eyes or mine
that see what we see channeling thought
from outside, that takes
the thought outside and covers
the things we see
someone else juggling what we see, two oranges
like two suns
from the window
        two knees under desk coming undone
the time I gave the reading and my hands were trembling
remember? and afterwards
it all came undone
I talked to you and outside

one went reeling down city streets
take the sun out of the sky and give it back to the streets
"back to mom's apron strings" and what we said about the sun
lit up our sky like a totem on a winter day
a holiday, but even the kids were gone
and one proceeded, stepping in the prints of those who had gone
new tracks in white, there was a serpent in the sky
who gave us permission not to mean the things we say
"if they meet in the open she must run away and hide"
"if they meet on a path she will throw herself
into the bushes"
there's the introvert
with an instinct for preserving time
the extrovert who's afraid of going inside
you can pick them out of a crowd and hold them up to the light
project them on the walls when the children are sleeping
and after they learn to walk, these children, you can look at them
with pride
in your eyes
since it goes without asking
crossing a river to the other side
a river, any body of water, I'd give my right arm to see
to stand on the bank
looking down from above
until the water overflows
"practicing the customs of our tribe"

5

What are the words? I wish I knew.
The words of greatness are in the song,
melting back into the things we did
or meant to do, the singer
not needed to make the words
seem true, but you won't know us

when we're gone. An island
is a gleaming star floating
on the sea. When I'm gone there'll
be the song, remember when
or that's what I did then, so now you can see,
I wasn't the person of whom you could say
love robbed him of his quickness or felicity
nor made him into the personification of a deity
by building statuettes at the entrances to the park
where kids might cry when they scraped their knees
running on asphalt in the dark.

6

The silence is a riddle
written in the grains of my desk,
which was here when I came
and replaced the desk that was lost,
that couldn't fill the space
of the room I lived in, was left behind,
and in its stead this wobbly board.
Are you bored by the silence? In the basement
there's a box of shoes worn by
the man who lived here
before, who called
to tell us his former wife and her
lawyer might come to the house when
he was gone, to appropriate it
like a song but we shouldn't let
them in, we're like caretakers who pay rent
but we musn't let the wife once adored
enter the house where she still gets mail we learn
because we also pick up the mail for this guy
whose box of shoes I found in a drawer.
Don't let the wife in. Don't let the lawyer

come through the door. Maybe we need an intermediary
to sift through things, possessions and what not, and tell
us what we can use to reward ourselves for
diligence in the field of capriciousness, free of enmity
cutting through our spiritual lives like a sword, fumbling
for coins and choosing the gold over the silver to proffer
the beggar who looks annoyed—later we see him
with a glass of wine on the banks of the fjord,
lost in the present while we look back to the past
which is smoky and dim lit rooms or rainy nights
waiting for a cab, afternoons of plane crashes read about
in tabloid headlines on street corner stands.
Our fantasies contradict our destinies, but they're the best
we have, when I was younger I did this—but it's all different now,
there's a scale on which we can chart the things we say
as a way of not worrying about the impressions we make,
gauge our reflections in the ripples of a lake, spreading out.

7

One's physical infirmities are acerbic, detachment's
a form of misogyny, I go to my books
vertiginously like a parrot screaming "Do your duty...."
I settle into the menagerie: exposed beams, rafters,
and a massive Louis XIV door over which I run my fingers.
The future invites me (as into
a sepulcher beneath the floor) and I follow, clumsily,
like the spirit of a dead man in the void.
I'm the absentee, the teacher's pet, a strange
character, a charter member: the one who waited
beneath a canopy in the rain until it was too late
to do anything but walk home alone. My shyness opens up
into a form of pigheadedness which dissolves
in lightheartedness. The waitress
tears out her hair, graying at the roots,

while the baby, practically bald,
drips yogurt onto the rug. A caul
(in which Byron was wrapped at birth) brings
good luck. Faint fumes of absinthe
and cigarettes fill the lungs. After
dinner we take our evening walk
down town roads leading downhill
while the light settles behind the trees
blurs, burrs, buds, burrows, beavers and bugs.

8

A baby nightgown
a "sleeper"
drips from the shower bar
to the bathroom floor

We do our laundry in the bathroom sink.
We don't go out to the laundromat anymore.
We wash our baby's
clothing by hand.

When the laundry
is done we hang it
up to dry
on the silver bar above the shower.

The local laundromat
isn't far,
in fact it's
just around the corner.

Every morning when
I brush my teeth
or shave,

I don't shave

every morning, the
bathroom sink
is filled with laundry
left over from the night before.

I take the stopper from the drain
—cold water disappears,
no suds remain—
rinse the clothing in the basin,

hang it
on the bar to dry.
I never want to go there anymore,
read magazines, and wait

for the laundry to dry.
No, I never want to go there
again, with you,
and wait for the laundry

and wait for the laundry.

9

Undressing and looking at my skin which is colorless
I remember the nuances of each hair on the surface
When the light catches it is a wheel of color spinning
Out of the circle and that there's nothing in the center
But the song of a starling

When I listen to the phone ring
I try not to wonder
If the effect of time

On the emotions
Is only an illusion
And if I answer
Against the backdrop
Of city streets
Will my voice recede
Down corridors
To escape the feelings I lost, or
Charge the clouds to be more
Personal than the words
I'm hearing? Did I say
All that once without really
Thinking
                 my words are part
Of the motif so I say them again
In intervals   of great importance
Delicate feminine tendencies   the dress of women
A personality without contrasts to be acquired over the counter
A human diversity, like a university of feeling, flying free
The things I meant to do, didn't do, did
Regretted later but never thought about after
Beguiling others by speaking in dulcet waves
Enamored of nothing but the world within

PAST ALL DISHONOR

We make waves. The clouds
roll by. Resiliency was never
my strength, and I won't bend
in the wind like a leaf or the trunk
of a tree just to get the message
from the stars, loud and clear,
or give up my heart to the feelings
in the air only because I'm alive,
and you are, and they're there. I'm
alive, it's true, but resiliency was
never my habitat, and change
was something I could only intuit
by smothering every new flower and plant,
by making each flower grow under a glass
bell as if for me alone, my pleasure
an unturned stone—we live in a backward
country now. I wheel the stroller
outside the bakery and when the kids
come out they're holding cookies
which the man behind the counter
gave them for free, in fact
every bakery you go into
the people who work there
give kids free cookies, even
babies are offered lollipops
without thinking that when the drug
enters the bloodstream my cells begin
to breathe and who wants habits anyway
like the cells of a leaf need chlorophyll
to turn green, and they do, and then they
turn yellow, and drop off
and die. We live in a backward country

now; our ideas are backward, 800,000 Palestinians
uprooted from the land they'd inhabited for 2000 years,
and you can't expect them just to drop what they were
doing and go away, and they were doing something—the
word "Arab" isn't a dirty word, its connotation
just tells me something about my own ignorance
of them, I can't be anti that or them,
I can't get lost inside a word like saying "she's
promiscuous" and then imagine her that way,
it's just a word that tells me nothing about them or her,
free from fear, insecurity, terror and oppression,
we live in a backward country now and you can't
expect it all to go away. My great-grandfather, and
namesake, Lewis Freedson, went to what's now Israel
in the 1920s, and in 1930 he died there, age 96,
and a few days ago a poet wrote me from Tel Aviv
asking me for poems so he could translate them
into Hebrew for an anthology of American poets to be
published in Israel, but today my ideas
are no longer sacrosanct, I'm Jewish but I don't want
to own all the words, I was born this way and I'm not
resilient but I'm not a creature of habit either,
I've been a poet for 20 years and I'm a father now, that's
enough constancy for one lifetime isn't it? My ideas
about these things won't go away: during 1948 500,000
to 800,000 Palestinians were forced
out of their country and off their
land—there's an illusion that we were
smarter than they were that was part of
the plan, that it didn't matter where they
went or what they did because we were better
than them, that was part of the plan then
but our ideas are open to doubt,
everything we did then must be questioned now,
we don't live in the same world we lived
in then, we're the backward country now,
I don't know anything about what it's like

to be an Arab but I imagine he
or she could determine his or her own fate if
asked, but no one was asked, and the people
who made the decisions for them have to be
questioned now, we can't put our fate in the hands
of the people who make the decisions for us now,
we may be moving backwards but our hearts are uncowed
and maybe you can't change the world over night
but you can say what you feel, free of insecurity and
oppression, no stigma attached to a tribe,
no privileged race, we live in a backward country
now, $600 a month for 4 rooms on the Lower East Side,
ignorance isn't bliss, my hand on the plow,
it's romantic to be a victim but I don't think
that way now, there are people and countries
are the places where they were born
and I think each person possesses a human heart
and a destiny which won't shatter over night
and if you're ignored long enough maybe you'll get up
and do something, and if I say: get out of here,
and it's your house, maybe you'll do something,
and maybe random acts of violence occur
because people are ignored and oppressed for so long
there's no other way, and I'd like to think
the goal is the same for everyone,
no heads or tails, no one loses, no black or white,
and if you want to sit down and talk things over
in what used to be thought of as a civilized way
let's understand that you came into my house
and told me to leave, that's where it began,
and I don't think you're any smarter or more advanced than
me, that was just something you thought without thinking
about me—my needs, my wants, my history—let's start
    from there.

WALKING THROUGH AIR

The door is still open but the guests have gone
Like shooting stars into the misty evening
And yet our thoughts of them linger on
And the memories they take from being with us
Every blemish frozen on a graph
Words someone said, someone meant to say, something forgot
Words left hanging in the air, that went by
Too quickly for a response to rise
Like smoke and register on the mind
Made memorable by nothing that was ever said
But what they thought about later in the end
At the end of their visit, footsteps echoing on the stairs.

The clouds went with them like feelings across the sky
And the heaven that was suddenly filled with stars
Reminded us that night had fallen while they were here,
Darkened windows, the lights of cars in the street
For whatever they are now thinking they are remembering us too
As if this visit was something dreamt and later revised
For accuracy's sake, to be invisible in our eyes.

Take into account how they secretly conspired
To say the opposite of what they meant
For what you forgot to tell them remains a mystery
(The brevity of the visit was no surprise)
And that the sum of what made them wise
Like a telegram to a person you love that was never sent
Sparked the only feelings they know how to convey
And what could we say but: how are you doing?

Bow down to your feelings as they come and go
Like friends, through a door and into the night
Like strangers who never entertained the thought of arriving

And to whom we said nothing, but hoped they enjoyed their trip
Through time, as if they'd known us in another time,
This is what we knew they were thinking.

So everyone departed at the same time, leaving us
To clean up as an afterthought in slow motion,
Assemble dishes on a tray and carry them to the kitchen.
Our thoughts of them are with us now, in separate diaries
We describe their visit, and later tonight,
Lying in bed, we'll compare notes as thoughts about
    what was meant
By words that were better left unspoken
Laughter, tears, our voices fill the air
An old emotion, commonplace sentiment everywhere.

OUT OF THE QUESTION

Don't think things out in your head
ahead of time. You know what
you're going to say before you do,
but not until you say it do you know it's true.
(The fact that you said it makes it true.)
In school I always knew the right answer.
When the teacher asked a question I formed the answer
in my head. By the time I'd rearranged
the words someone else had answered the question.
(It's not necessary to know what you're saying
before you do.) "It's just on the tip of my tongue,"
someone said, and it's true,
the tip of the tongue contains the answer.
Much in the same way the painter's brain
is in her wrist, so the answer lies elsewhere, not
where you think. (The answer lies elsewhere, not
where you think.) "Do I think these words
as I write them?" is a good question.
Sometimes I say them aloud to myself.
I read what I've written aloud, without thinking.
(The words in the air are in my head.)

                    One way of getting to know people
is to ask them questions. "Where were you born?" is a
    good example
of a question that doesn't require much thought.
(Once when I asked someone a question, she asked, in return,
whether I was really interested i.e. did the answer matter?
wasn't I just making small talk? passing the time? as if to imply
we might as well go to bed together without talking,
it was inevitable no matter what either of us said.
And later I thought that maybe she was right: the present
exists outside ourselves, where it's happening, not in our heads.)

The present exists in some kind of here and now
where what I'm saying no longer matters. If you say
what you don't mean, then apologize afterwards,
feel remorse, write a letter or make a call—the words
you spoke without thinking are in the air,
like wrong answers or wrong numbers
when a stranger answers. Remember
the nursery rhyme about how words couldn't
harm you? Well, it isn't true.

Some teachers become frightened if they think
one of their students knows more about the subject
in question than they do, while other teachers
discourage students from forming their own opinions.
Still other teachers treat everyone they meet like students.
They judge you by the way you talk about what you do.

You ask a question, you get an answer. "Ask me no questions
and I'll tell you no lies." Neither a borrower nor a lender be etc.
Some people like to talk, while others look attentive,
sitting up straight in their chairs like they learned at school.
(To break the silence you ask a question: "What's on your mind?"
and someone answers.)

And someone answers. Didn't we know that all the time?
In every question there's an answer implied, as
in every thought there's a horse without blinders
running across the broken cobblestones of the past,
down the street where the trolley used to pass
and where the tracks still remain, trailing his wagon behind.
Didn't the mind go blank for a moment, my mind
when you asked the question and I turned to speak
not knowing it was you at first, saying nothing
because I didn't understand what you said, amazed
it was you and that we were alone together gathering

our thoughts into words which would then light up
if not the space between us, then the entire world?

I know some questions have answers linking the questions
to questions that were answered by things that were said
in the past, and that the world we light up goes around in
circles like what happened last year or where were we then,
that our lives turn into a kind of monster with a hundred
arms and heads, the monster of kindness that turns our heads
into a single flower or a patch of green where the snow melted
over night into spring's harbinger, and that taking all this for
     granted
we resume our positions at the windows we look out on
     disturbing the night
with the questions that remain to be asked, having come this far.

PRECIOUS METTLE

One ends in ignominy because one begins mistakenly
virtue is angelic and vice makes us meek
we haven't drawn the lines around our hearts so clearly
it's impossible to say "no" to love, or anything,
easy to imitate nature but what part of nature should we choose
the face of the passing stranger who runs his fingers along your
    sleeve
I think I'd like a drink but I don't have any money
the perversity of a tree whose leaves forgot to bloom
should we imitate the sky or go to our room
where the stars painted on the ceiling revolve in time to the music
which imitates our fears of feeling too much without knowing
if it's love of ourselves which makes us feel weak,
a person fainting at dawn on the street,
the scars of the person beside you in bed,
I trace your face with my fingers and you awaken
to the touch, pornographically speaking I love you less
or too much, deformed by wickedness like all of life
if one can define wickedness as the way other people think
and who can remember the night in December
we walked hand in hand through the empty streets
struck dumb by the snow as it fell on our faces
this wasn't hell, but the outer traces
you paid your tab at the grocery on 6th
I bought a pack of smokes for the journey

THE LITTLE MATCH GIRL

She's the sometime lover of someone's
best friend, but I don't know her well. No
one writes "Fuck Manny" on the wall of
the elevator anymore. "There are men
born to greatness, but I am not one of
them" (Clement Atlee). She's someone
I don't know well at all except
what I learn when other people talk
about her. They say so and so called
and she said this or that. Once
I called up a girl named Timberlake but
her mother answered and I didn't leave
my name. Germans and Anglo-Saxons
don't kiss you goodbye, hello; the French
and the Italians are usually more effusive.
She looks at me and then I look away.
She might be someone I might have married
had I known her long ago. She sees me coming
and turns the other cheek. That imbecile
building is constructed out of names,
like an icicle, but the names are
unmentionable in polite conversation.
We still say "fuck you" to the cars when
they don't stop. I suppose that for some
people arguing is a form of intimacy.
I think people pay money in order to suffer
i.e. sometimes the pleasure doesn't seem worth
the effort. Something makes pleasure feel
ordinary, and at peace with itself,
not bottled up or held back or helpless
because something that happened when you
were a kid made you feel that way, the way you
are now. I met a girl from Dalton in

Washington Square Park but when I asked
her out on the phone she said "I'm sorry."
Neither a cough nor love can be concealed.
A high tree is a symbol of scopophobia,
scars never disappear, and the fantasy
of rebirth is often a substitute for
intercourse with mother, father, or someone.
She seems to be avoiding me lately and it worries
me that a feeling can die before it even begins,
like any plant from lack of sunlight or nourishment.
A piece of chocolate cream pie might
make me feel better. The penetrating
eye detects jealousy in every corner; the
complacency of a person who's done too well
generates hubris; clear heads are not
enough—it's dangerous to be happy. What
is the outlet for those who can't think clearheadedly
projecting unwanted feelings in the light on the wall
which casts its own shadow like a messenger
but not from heaven but from above heaven and the rays
of sun are thunderbolts to us mortals
who can't even speak to each other on the
phone without thinking what if her mother answers
and she isn't there, what will I say?
Not the intensity but the duration
of feelings, I know all about that.
But if something lasts 5 minutes or 5 days and then fades away
who's to say it was any less? as
long as the memory of it stays the same,
and it does. "I'm sorry, but I'm busy
Friday night," doesn't mean you shouldn't
try me again. I didn't, I wouldn't, I
don't—I can barely detach the voice
in my throat from whatever makes me
talk but I won't show that to someone
I don't even know just so she can reject me

in all my fear and nakedness, it isn't worth it
if I'm going to give so much and have it fall
on deaf ears. Oh, why am I so sensitive?
I don't think I'll ever take the incentive again.
I'll just follow after somebody and wait to see
what happens, it's easier that way.
She has so many pockets—filled with match-
books, silk and lace—who can decide
where to look first? It's dawn, and I've
been awake too long, the window goes
blond slowly and I feel like I'm being born
again, an urchin under the falling snow
which makes everything—tops of cars
and sides of buildings—seem unfinished
as the scene shifts inside and I find myself alone.
She thinks that on the day of Resurrection someone, God,
will count up her worst deeds and reward her for
what she did best, but she doesn't say this
in so many words. "A chair is meant
to be sat in, music is good for
what it does to you, love is sleeping
together, hate is wanting to kill…" I can't
say it's her voice or mind that
interests me, that would be too
mundane. I can't say I like her
stockinged feet, a diamond brooch, a
string of pearls, the cameo
enclosing a portrait in its lapis
folds, the pigment of color that touches
her cheeks. I can't say I like
the way she walks, and is forgotten,
a whole person, or admire the effortless
way she comes of age, blooming over night
like a star or a flower, as one might say.
Sometimes I think it would make a difference
if I knew something about her she didn't know

I knew. Then I could surprise her
by acting coy and supercilious
simultaneously, watch the shadow
of innocence as it fades from
her face, as I—in my innocent way,
and as if nothing were amiss—overstepped even
the bounds of joy and bliss, just to provide
a platform for my feelings, and steal a kiss.

KOREAN LOVE SONG

There's a photo in my locket
of my lover which I'll treasure
forever even though he never
thinks of me, and working long hours

behind a counter gives
me pleasure, I see the sweep
of the branches of the original
tree, the luminous echo

of being a part of someone's
presence, and I fall asleep
inside the deep sigh of gratitude
which lingers like the trace

of down on my knee.
When I see women luxuriate
in expensive dresses
I think of how little

I need to feel
happy, and when I kiss the ground
it opens at my feet.
There's a place where it's warmer

that looks like a dagger
on the map which I trace
with the tip of my finger,
but I don't want to go there

without my family,
even though I'm older
and don't need an escort

to walk down the street.

When I place my finger
to my lips it means, be still.
When I unbutton my blouse
your illusions are shattered,

and soothing words won't give
order to the silver lining
of your dreams. Just because
I'm someone's daughter doesn't

mean I won't kill.
Love is more than
the measure of feeling,
an omen so strong

even the birds
stop singing. They
eat the crumbs
from my hands

then fly off. At the sound
of a gun or a car backfiring
they disperse. Why
settle for anything less

than perfect freedom?
Why not fly, like the
birds, to someone else's
arms? Mine are too much

like the arms of the angel
who never returned
to heaven when she was
summoned to the throne

but who stayed
in the stone garden
and followed the frayed
edge of her lover's coat

as he stretched out
beneath the trees
and made a tent
for her to sleep in.

Now I won't accept anyone's
money in payment for love
even though I'm poor
and my lover's gone.

His photo in my locket is all I have
to remind me of the nights we spent together.
Perhaps he's lying in someone
else's bed or on an open patio

beneath the stars, with someone
else's dress draped
over the back of a chair.
I don't care. The imagination

plays too many tricks
and if love means being in
another person's skin
for a minute, that's what we had.

Maybe someday I'll
return to the garden
with a new lover,
unbutton my blouse

and feel the air
against my skin,
and when the darkness
descends on the opposite shore

I'll get down
on my hands and knees
in the dirt
and beg for more.

THE CORSET

"To the Slaves of Fashion"

You must try and lace me tighter, lace me tighter, mother dear;
My waist, you know, is nearly half the size it was last year;
I will not faint again, mother, I care not what they say,
Oh! it's sixteen inches today, mother, it's sixteen inches today.

There's many a wee, wee waist they say, but none so wee as mine;
I'm five-foot-five-and-a-half in height, my inches forty-nine;
Last year my waist was—Oh! Its size I'd be afraid to say,
But it's sixteen inches today, mother, it's sixteen inches today.

You must lace me tight tonight, mother, I must try and keep this size,
I know the doctors tell you it is dangerous—unwise,
And they call me vain and foolish, but I care not what they say,
For it's sixteen inches today, mother, it's sixteen inches today.

I stay so quiet all day, mother, afraid the cords might burst,
I can breathe quite freely now, though it hurt me so at first;
At first it hurt me very much, but now I'm happy and gay
For it's sixteen inches today, mother, it's sixteen inches today.

You remember the first month, mother, what agony I bore,
But I went through it without flinching; the corsets that I wore
Measured seven-and-twenty inches; Oh I care not what they say,
For it's sixteen inches today, mother, it's sixteen inches today.

I

A narrowness of waist betrays a narrowness
of mind

II

The claim that women
had discarded their
corsets towards the
end of the 19th century
had about as much
truth as the boast
that they had burned
their bras in the 1960s

III

This kind of garter
was to keep the corset
from riding up
on the hips

IV

A new and exceedingly simple
fastening secures the front, and a
concealed spring prevents the
opening of the lowest stud

V

Young girls should be prohibited
from sitting cross-legged

VI

Shop-assistants tight-lace
in order to attract customers
and increase sales

VII

It is reported that women
have laced men to death

VIII

At Hupfenhelm during an official
ball given by the mayor, the virtuous
but excessively tight-laced Fräulein
Rosamvade Yheg suddenly exploded
after the fifth allemande,
with a detonation that broke
all the windows of the town and
with such violence that her limbs
were hurled across the hall,
killing two students including one who
was beheaded by the flying busk

IX

The Divorce Corset
did not refer to marital
disagreement but to the separation
of one breast from the other
by means of a padded
triangle of iron and steel

X

Death fantasies cannot
be excluded from tight-
lacing psychology

XI

Tight-lacers attempt to measure the pain threshold

XII

Speculation upon the psychological basis
for the gratification offered by tight corsets
has tended to be biased by a puritan prejudice

XIII

Tight-lacing was
viewed as a guarantee
of fidelity
        and as a means
of prolonging sexual interest

at a time when it tended
to wear thin

XIV

Threading and un-
threading, pulling in
and out at various
points in different
degrees and in a certain
sequence, the reducing,
closing and leaving of gaps

XV

"se déclasser"   (to relax)
"se délacer"   (to unlace oneself)

XVI

The state of being tightly corseted
constitutes ipso facto
a demand for erotic release

XVII

The husband fumbled confusedly
with the lacing of his bride's corset

XVIII

The tight-lacer justifies herself
to her lover
            on the grounds that
he would be the first to complain
if she didn't enjoy being squeezed

XIX

The footman
is more potent
and attractive
than the husband

XX

Admit a low-class
male servant, rather than a lover,
to the intimacy
                of a sacred ritual

XXI

When lacing became tight-lacing
one of the means of degrading it socially
was to suggest that it necessitated the muscle-power
of the male lover servant

XXII

With the front-fastening corset, the

time and effort formerly spent
putting in the laces could be spent
on tightening them

XXIII

The front-fastening steel busk,
which saved one the trouble of removing
the lace completely, and then recorseting
it at each wearing, diminished
the ritual in which a maid or
lover was the active participant

XXIV

The erotic symbolism of the front busk diminished
when it was split in two

XXV

As late as the early
20th century
                it was the custom
for a Sicilian bridegroom
to present a hand-carved busk
to his bride

XXVI

The stiffening agency of the corset
was concentrated in the busk

XXVII

Around 1900 the girdle
began to cover the pubic area
and furnish an actual obstacle,
like the legendary chastity belt,
to penetration

XXVIII

The waist-oppressive corset
has always stopped short of the pubic area

XXIX

The hard armor seems to protect
the vital organs located in the thorax
and abdomen
                    but insofar as it stops short
of the sexual nodes i.e.
                        nipples and genitals
it also serves to expose her sexual vulnerability
and enhance the softness of her (exposed)
breasts and thighs

XXX

Even as she induces sexual temptation
a woman is seemingly armored against it

XXXI

The extra tight-laced corset
is a means of exercising control
while enhancing the provocation

XXXII

"Tight" and "stiff" are
words which embody ancient
hierarchical associations
with control, duty, morality,
rank etc.

XXXIII

In adopting the collar, women
were transferring to the neck
a form of construction to which
they had already been conditioned
at the waist and the feet

XXXIV

The stiff collar is identified as
a symbol of duty as well as
phallic erection

XXXV

The collar protects
an area in the male

vulnerable to an enemy
weapon or disease

XXXVI

The woman who unties the man's tie
may be making a sexual invitation

XXXVII

Elimination of abdominal
in favor of pectoral breathing
creates movement about the breasts
which may be constantly
palpitating with desire

XXXVIII

The open-legged
position has always
been regarded
as potentially indecent

XXXIX

As in high heels, the corset
creates a dynamic
between restriction and movement

XL

The illusion of a body in
a permanent state of sexual
excitation

XLI

Flattened breasts have never established
themselves in the Western tradition,
as they have in Asia

XLII

In the 16th through 18th centuries
breast-flattening served to emphasize
breadth of hips

XLIII

The "uplift" obtained by modern
brassiere engineering was earlier
achieved by the corset

XLIV

Little Chinese girls, learning to walk
again after their feet were first bound,
were explicitly warned against the bad
habit of poking out their chins

XLV

Opponents of high heels have
stressed the ungainly thrusting
forward of the chin by
the inexperienced high-heel wearer

XLVI

While there are women
who walk more securely
in high heels than their
sisters in low or no
heels, and there are those
whose locomotion in high
heels is an aggressive
appropriation of space and time,
the contrary and complementary
associations are with precariousness
and imbalance, the appeal for a
supporting arm, the promise
of imminent fall, surrender

XLVII

The popularity of classical ballet and other
forms of tip-toe dance in the 19th century
represents a major public, artistically sublimated
manifestation of foot and leg fetishism

XLVIII

Slenderness of
heel has

weapon-related
sado-masochistic
associations
heightened by
sharpness of
toe ("stiletto"
heel)

XLIX

The Chinese idea of a foot
small enough to fit inside
a man's mouth probably
reflects an oral-genital fantasy

L

Permanent compression of the
foot was believed to induce
a kind of walk which
enlarged the hips

LI

Gallant males rushed
to their rescue with 20
pocket knives which they used
to cut corset strings
as the quickest remedy
for collapsed lungs

LII

A California boy can be jailed for twelve years
as a dangerous sex criminal for privately masturbating

LIII

A perverted interest in
women's underwear recently
resulted in the murders
of several women

LIV

Jail is the proper place for men
who like to sit in shoe shops
watching women try on shoes

LV

Apart from footwear, criminal
fetishists were involved with
gloves, handkerchiefs and hair-depilation

LVI

The study of fetishism was motivated by the desire
to erase it

LVII

In an Austrian poem of 1890
the pain of a girl's love is equated
with the pain of a corset

LVIII

The preacher tells how
he chanced upon a corset
lying on a table

LIX

The extreme contraction
of the lower ribs

LX

The sucking in of
the belly appears as the
primary physiological
indication of sacrificial
agony

LXI

North European late Gothic art
has used extreme narrowness of waist
to convey the purity and suffering
in figures of Christ and the saints

LXII

The word "fetish"
derives from the Portuguese
feitico

LXIII

The true tight-
lacing fetishist
does not wish
to possess the corset
but to apply it
possessively
upon the body
of the beloved

LXIV

Tight-lacing fetishism
is not the same as corset
fetishism

LXV

Fetishists
pioneered
multiple
piercing
along
the ear rim

LXVI

True fetishists generally
avoid medical visits

LXVII

Pressure-marks increase
epidermal sensitivity
for erotic purposes

LXVIII

Scarification effects are
prized by some who
admire the visual impression
of the criss-cross
pressure marks left by
the boning and laces of a corset

LXIX

For a long time the
only clinical studies of
female fetishism
concerned satin
and silk kleptomaniacs

LXX

Lingerie is decorative and passive, or extremely
active

LXXI

The post-war admiration
for largeness of bust has
replaced that for smallness
of waist and extremities

LXXII

Until recently the big
bust was regarded as
a virtue in itself

LXXIII

Surgical breast reduction
is also on the increase

LXXIV

Breast-flattening is always associated
with the waistless, corsetless Twenties
but it is also characteristic of the 16th
and 17th centuries when the whole thorax
was rigidly encased

LXXV

Any form of décolletage
was already offensive

from AVENUE OF ESCAPE

TRAVELOGUE

To merely uncover the depths of love
By sitting here same spot establishes dignity
No more submissive than he was to his mother
A love forgotten but the lover's body remains
A ring of pure light circles the earth every hour
The point from which you begin to distort what you're trying
    to say
My imaginary brother follows me like a shadow
The woman upstairs says she thinks her dog found something
    that resembles a gerbil and ate it
Nietzsche was fun to read in prison
You can't love something that doesn't exist
The church, family, a tree whose branches fell off in the storm
No one will punish you if you feel too much pleasure
It's not cold outside but inside—it's like winter
What I saw when I looked down at the woman and her lover
    was a reflection of the shadow of the heart broken
    into shards
The agency of the letter moves through the fabric of fate
I had a crush on my neighbor but she moved out of town
The dress is made of cotton—it's really a jumper
How to hold a stranger at arm's length and comfort him?
The strangest part was when there was no place to go,
    no home, and I had to sit on stoops, out-doors,
    or loiter in shops, linger in restaurants over glasses
    of iced coffee and mint tea
Unable to speak the language of the Cantonese waitress
    whose job was "off the books" and whose livelihood
    depended on the amount of money I tipped her
Everything derives from a lack of attention, broken span
    into which something drops
Depending on the day of the week or your mother I love you,
    hate you more some days

I stand on the edge of town, light burning in the window
I drive through hopeless Canada, aching with dignity
I walk into the bodega and buy a lightbulb and a loose cigarette
A transparency of hair catches the flame of his first desire
They met in 1965 and lived together 4 years
Dark hallway filled with guys I don't know, smoking
I've saved some dinner, all I have to do is heat it up
When she returns from her job she neither kisses me nor says
    hello
The people who cut through the fog with scythes went
    on strike
Desire overcomes inertia, but the stones survive

THE OUTER BANKS

You could say that characters in The Bible were obsessed
    with hiding their nakedness

I touch the leg of the table with the toe of my foot

The child searches in a drawer for the damaged toy

Feelings of love were impaired by excessive anxiety

I put in my order with the butcher before it gets too late
    and the holidays are "upon us" or so they say

You can wear the same clothing every day and no one cares

She complains that she spends too much time making herself
    beautiful while he just picks up the clothing he
    wore yesterday from the floor and doesn't even
    bother washing his face or combing his hair

I hear a rooster cry at dawn from someone's roof

I experience an epiphany, I'm not what you might call handy

There's a dead seal on the beach and a fishing boat on the horizon

The guy downstairs complains about a leak when I take a shower

Some people don't mind if you take them for granted

She can't break up with her boyfriend until she knows
    she has another waiting in the wings

It's hard to love anyone who holds a grudge

I wear my compromises over my mask

My deficiencies won't add up, no ice no drink

The shades of night toss their dilapidated forms over my
    shoulders like a Ukrainian shawl

Women with kerchiefs, a family with stroller, her equestrian
    thoughts ride into the sunset

Think of A's love for B in terms of the needs of A for whom
    B provides the promise of immediate gratification

The sun goes down in my mirror where I address myself not as
    "I" but as a you who exists outside me and can't think

I thought I'd take time out from my work to make a call
    but as soon as I heard her voice I hung up

A 16-year old student has been charged as an adult with
    attempted murder and unlawful use of a weapon in the
    shooting of a teacher who ordered him to stop smoking

Seek out a stranger to alleviate desire but don't call her
    back—she might be "busy tonight"

It seems like you might as well have a drink to loosen you up

In the summer of 1964 I lived in a bungalow in Far Rockaway
    with my girlfriend, her father and her baby

"She's not here now—she's never here—who should I say called?"

It strikes me: it strikes me that I repeat everything twice in
    my life, and keep repeating, without acknowledging my
    mistakes

Some people keep love at a distance because they're frightened of
    being hurt but it's hard to be on the outside looking in at
    your own life or perpetually standing on the edge of
    things with nowhere to go

We thought the matinee began at 3 but when we arrived it was
    intermission

People meet on a blind date and eventually get married for the
    sake of discretion ("my parents wanted me to")

You find out what interests you, but don't do it—not yet,
    anyway—since it's more interesting to put it all off
    till tomorrow, to let things slide, to trap the thought
    in its beauty like a tiger in a cage and watch it climb the
    walls and disfigure itself out of sheer helplessness

You map out a theory of knowledge and watch it dissolve like an
    integer divided by itself, but turned on their sides
    the numbers look like songs

You pretend to work hard so others will leave you alone

You talk to strangers and megalomaniacs, you read books you
    read before

You prefer pieces of paper with words on them to people, but
    that phase passes

You identify with the tree outside your window: all my family
    makes a home here but the branches are obscure even
    to me

You sing a judicious symphony like a necklace of amber beads

A half-dressed man leans out the window and shouts to his
    girlfriend on the sidewalk

A police car with a loudspeaker announces a reward for any
    information leading to the arrest and convction of a person
    who shot a policeman

I was working in the library at Columbia University and we met
    during my lunch hour on the steps of Grant's Tomb

Tumblers on the tray bisect the light of the immigrant wafer
    which we place on the tongue to taste the snow, the rain
    and the spray which from yonder fountain alights on our
    faces

There's a bracelet close to her skin that resembles ivy but if
    I touch it I fear my heart might grow numb

The specialty of the house wasn't on the menu but you could
    request it from the waiter, waitress or maitre d' who
    would bow down and kiss your knees out of a desire to
    give pleasure

Love is no solution to fear, the touch of a hand in the dark,
    nor the flowers, nor the beating of the wings against
    the screen

A job that represses your sexual instincts may be just what
    you need

"Don't wait up for me" is something I might have said
    but when I returned the bed was a talisman
    of crumbs and plaster

They say there was a lot of rain and possible flooding before
    we came: they tell us we brought the bad weather with us

Tell us what remains of desire, as you know it

All the swings in the park are taken, all the benches broken,
     let's sit here

There's a jail across the border where they'll take us when
     we get out of hand and from which we can see the evening
     star, a symbol of the persistence of desire

All they can do is torture us, behold us in wonder at our
     beauty, desiring to subjugate us because we're so unlike
     them in our sweet ways, and even our most muddled
     intuitions are wiser than the vows of militancy they
     concoct

I go to the prison of the practical world to take care of business

I look up my name in the index but it isn't listed

She was born and died before my time but if she were alive
     today we might have been pals

Bodies intermingle in a subway car—I stare covertly at legs,
     arms, eyes

I collect the wood and light the coals, but the wood is wet and I
     have to use a whole box of blue tips just to keep
     it going

I plant the symbol of order, Neptune's trident, on the opposite
     side of the archipelago and set forth under warm skies to a
     new terrain, spellbound by the possibilities of the future
     and the shadows of the strange birds hanging motionless
     on the horizon, but I don't know the name of the boat
     I'm aboard—it's like a shadow of some other boat
     that went down in the storm off the Isle of Good Hope,

where promises of love were made only to be broken
the next day, where marriage vows were spoken
in the shadows of an empty cathedral, where friends
and relatives gathered to wish you well—could
anyone of them, or you, predict
this spell of cold weather
we've been having recently?

All the objects in the world won't unlock the door to the
     present where daylight strips us of night's desire
     and a voice riding the airwaves whispers into the fog:
     Don't lose heart

When I close my eyes I can see the after-image of the light
     of the candle like the face in a dream, you are my
     shadow

DIFFERENT TRAINS

1

I'm coming home
in the rain with
no excuses,
I'm late
it's late in
the day to
give lies
credence, to
believe one's
own lie
(but I was just
talking to
myself), to
strike a nerve
alive with
the desire to
speak the truth,
to unnerve meaning
through clenched
teeth and open
eyes

2

I was brought up with a distorted
view of heaven. Took it to bed with me
but couldn't sleep. It was like
going to the store when my mother
asked and returning with the change in
my sweaty palm. Should I drop the coins

into the jar on the table in the foyer?
Heart says "yes," body can't decide.
My mother says "Is that you?"
as I walk through the gate.

3

The wind came off the page and embraced
me. And then the words of the author
embraced me as well. The wind blew the
pages forward and back. I lost my place,
I forgot what I was reading. Usually,
when I stop reading, I fold down the
corner of the page to mark my place.
I removed my reading glasses and put on
the glasses I wear to see distances.
I placed the book on the ground at my
feet and watched the wind rifle the
pages. I balanced the open book against
the stump of a tree and watched the wind
blow through the pages until all the
words were erased. I fell asleep in my
chair with a book open on my knees.

4

Who put the words inside your mouth?
They weren't there when I saw
you last. Someone speaking in capital

letters, surface thoughts (an
endless diatribe of anger and regret).
I'll probably die regretting not doing

this, don't you think? It's no joke growing old
in a place where there's nothing
to do. But I like the climate

of doubt that melts into parallel
lines and the fantasy of loving
two people at the same time.

5

There's another way of seducing someone
into doing what you want. A heart
blasted into space without
precaution, in the next life
you'll focus all your energy on
one person (if it kills you). If
I spoke (spontaneously) from the heart
I knew I could get her attention. Also,
it's possible to seduce someone
without even trying. Everyone
wants to seduce her but me.
Isn't that interesting?

6

Don't raise me to the heights
and then discard, that's all I ask.
Don't buffet an obsession so flimsy,
my nightgown caught on a nail.
The soul isn't responsible
for what it says. The grammar
of monotony when I see her coming.

7

Laura was sitting in the living room
watching television trying not to listen
to the sounds Janice and Bill were making
in the bedroom. Janice had asked Laura
whether she minded if Bill came home with
her and Laura didn't have the heart to tell
her that Bill had called every night that
week when Janice was at work. "It's just a
matter of time," he told Laura, "before Janice
and I break up." Laura didn't particularly care
whether they broke up or not. She was dozing
off when Bill came into the living
room with a towel wrapped around his waist.
He knelt on the rug and lifted her skirt
and she spread her legs so that her ankles were resting
on his shoulders "You can scream
all you want," he said. "She's asleep."

8

The letter arrives
like an arrow
crossing the margin
of destiny, but
no one has the nerve
to break the seal.

I have neither tenure
nor benefits. My mother
gives birth to a laurel
branch in a dream.
Mild-mannered, well-meaning,
temper and cool.

9

words reverberate like
recently sharpened pencils
to address the air
they float through

sequin desert mirage
embody a season
without end

Once I lived in a house
with a pantry where I kept
a 40-pound bag of potatoes
and some jam jars in case
I wanted to drink some jam

you can tell whether a poem's
any good by the type of paper
it's printed on

not *Remembrances of Things Past*
but a memory of wasted time

here, at the drawing board, gnawing
a bone

the taboo about a bone
eating human flesh also
a tattoo about a rose, the eye
of the gorgon, someone's mother

Sex, not work: but
you're fired, we've hired
someone else

where I am you said you'd be
it was my father's promise

Amor equals action: I think
I crossed this bridge before. A
firefly alights on the hem
of her dress.

an earring so weighted with pleasure
it touches my shoulder
                                    a gift of speech
tokenism   but I am present
in this form alone

10 *Phaedra*

His erudition is daunting, but all
he can do is spout indifference
to my own concerns, which only concern him
in as much as he's in front of me
(can I ask him to kneel?), and how to make
myself apparent, even nude I'm unvarnished,
so that suicide might be one way to trip the real
                                    and find him wanting.

11

Every place is the same. You can't
travel far enough away from yourself
to make it seem any different. Sometimes
I fly away but only half of me is there,
disengaged from the part of me that
remained on the ground. I'm here—but
I'm remembering what it felt like to be

in that place. It feels like floating,
like flying in a plane, like looking
down. The farther I go the more I feel
I've been somewhere else, but
it's useless to cry out when you're
lost in space, a dot filling a hole
that didn't exist before you came.
They reserve a place for you, and you fill it,
overjoyed at being accepted,
but it's only a vague sense of longing
that keeps the plane soaring above the ground.
A feeling of antipathy lingers in the air.
I get off the plane and no one's there.

12

All my words add up to a single
thought, don't you know? But
sometimes not thinking in words I
lose sight of the meanings.

Here is a set of rules
to justify your existence: we
all follow the same rules but
we can't depend on the sacraments

as instruments of salvation
to become someone we already
know. The idea that you can
depend on someone to respond

to your feelings was absorbed
into the idea of loss
that had nothing to do
with this person. No one

can gratify your need to
be loved. It's rare to find
one other person to fulfill
all your needs. All you can do

is focus your attention on one
other person and hope for the best.
All you can do is bury your head
under the blankets and weep

13 *for Sophia*

Climb up the side of
a statue for a view
of the city, don't fall

The houses that seemed to be
out of reach, the entrance
to the subway where you retie
your shoe in luxury

Even the view of the river
a dead man's rattle
strikes a chord
in your feverish heart

Or so I told you
as you were starting
out: stay calm
cross at the corners

in perfect visibility

14

A mirror at the bottom of the world,
reflecting our arms and faces. A newspaper
on the table, unread. The television
turned down low or unplugged. The door
closed between rooms. The cat scratching
at the door, wanting in. A prescription,
the name of a doctor, a vial of pills.
A photograph of myself and my children on
a lake in the country ten years ago. All
words, my voice, the beginning and end
of a sentence. A person listening to what
I say, a shock of disbelief on her face.
The body in bed: at rest or asleep. A cup
of tea cooling on the bedside table.

15

Nothing dominates silence like words
A derelict subscription to a magazine of poetry
The pages hiss with phrases like "despite this"
    and "togetherness"
Which we memorize and recite
Till the tea kettle whistles

Even the man selling incense on the subway platform
Rubs the back of his neck, his ego tightens
Like a caress
At the crash of dominoes

I thought of the correctness of an attitude
To pleasure that would take into account
The domino effect of words collapsing
Into one another

The lines of the page were like the rungs of a ladder
Leading to heaven, and I was the medium
Through which they flowed back to earth

16

I went to bed with Providence but we didn't
fuck. "I like to make love, not fuck," she said,
to which I responded: "I like to do both."
Sometimes we walked to the outskirts of the city
and took pictures of dumps, diners, abandoned
garages. My convictions are real but I'm easily
discouraged. For nourishment all I need is a ration
of servitude, the futile anxiety (stop) between
(stop) stupor and frenzy, a trunk steeped with
soiled bibs. All I knew of her past was what
she told me in her sleep. You could say this was
the raison d'être, in the old-fashioned sense,
for being alive, to be one of those for whom
happiness comes as easy as breath, but I'd be
lying to myself if I thought we could last forever,
that one night, as we lay in bed with the blankets
on the floor, hair matted to the silk pillowcase,
the cops aren't going to arrive with their clubs
and accoutrements and cart us away in the back
of their tiny trucks.

17

The truth of loving is knowing
it might someday end but it doesn't
prevent you from saying "I'll
never love anyone again." In the
giving up of who you are to

someone else, in the forgetting
of oneself, in the feeling
that you might strangle a person
out of love, that sweat can intermingle
so freely, the vortex of anonymity in
a stranger's kiss, is this a sin? I woke
up (I was talking in my sleep) on the
kitchen floor, the notes of "Für
Elise" drifting through an open window.
I was getting around all right
by myself, or so I thought (I even
held some love in reserve for the other
in case she returned). If you want
to take a giant step forward you have to
say "please" or "May I?" lest you go
back to the beginning and repeat
your mistakes. You don't want
to hear what it feels like to be
me (separate from you) and who
can blame you? This fragment was
only something of what was possible,
a clearing in the densest wood, but
it's pointless to think of what
might have been: if no one
gives anything there's nothing
to have to begin with. Sacrificing
everything, without holding
back, and then making it happen
again. The giving up of who
you are to another, the giving in.

18

I know that somewhere it's written
in bold type on yellow parchment
for everyone to read, but the signature
an X on a line changes intermittently
and with some humor, so that bathing
stepping up out of the bath where
everything descends, is part
of what I miss, what I'm blocking out.
The story, I miss you, every few inches
another window, and you're looking back
at me from the ledge, bird-like, alive
to what's most real, the cars
on the parkway, no longer alive
to what I can almost feel
is you, listening and breathing
in the other room. Sobs intermittent
keys on a chain, to adore you, no
to be impervious to your adoration.
To dominate is not to adore in pain.
No thought as impervious as the
clouds are, a natural wonder,
no longer exempt from suffering, but free—
and the air yields.

A MAN ESCAPED

Words escape through gaps:
meaning converts them into conduits.
Stained leaves. Dyed parchment
on which nothing is crossed out.
The words begin to swagger through the
whiteness of a last refrain,
then draw back, seductive, as if no
longer responsible, compromising
themselves like a series of defective vehicles
that have to be shipped back to the factory
from the dealership window.
Invective in a starling's mouth,
refracting pleasure down to the last decibel.

GRACE NOTES

But losing out, losing
one hair out of
the darkness, losing
the thread of
conversation, simply

losing one's way and
winding up
in a forest
with others like you—
has nothing to do

with loss of love
identity loss and speech loss,
the loss of one's lover,
what it felt like
to be young. It has

little to do with
seeing the world through
a monocle, or rekindling
your feelings so
you can live

among the trolls.
The desiccated glass
feeds on the reflection
of an open door, a voice
in the other room,

footsteps, the turn of a key.
We listen at the confessional
for the progress of materialism

to set an example, but we won't
lift a cudgel to the door

of the sanctuary. In time,
pleasure finds an empty
carriage for our posthumous
songs. Can a bird petition mythology
for a place in the pantheon?

Will we ever stop doting?

ENTERING NIGHT

There are fences around churches to keep the agony from steeping

I wash the dishes by starlight, it's all I can do for today

You get the impression people are laughing at him behind his
    back and that he doesn't care

Someday I'll come back to this street and say: I used to live here

The American woman in the Japanese restaurant opened her
    blouse and massaged her breast as she talked to her
    boyfriend who slouched in his chair

Won't order any new food in restaurant for fear I won't like it—
    order only what I like another ruined evening

They tell you it can't last because they don't want you to be
    happy, people are like that I'm afraid

Don't think I'm being withdrawn if I seek refuge in my private
    world

I used to play "Für Elise" but then I told my piano teacher
    I wanted to play "popular" music so he brought
    me the score for "The King and I" and I quit taking lessons

All we could do when we got to the park was sit on the grass, eat
    sandwiches, play ball

And so much to say, how long can I linger over this letter, among
    the boxes of tea and sweeteners, don't take everything
    for yourself

Before putting on mascara comb through and separate eyelashes
   with an old toothbrush

You could hope for an act of generosity that wasn't someone's
   idea of a deal, an exchange over a counter for some
   commodity like the elixir of life

I know better than to think I'd debase my own feelings by letting
   them stagnate like weeds at the bottom of a lake without
   first tearing them up from the roots with my bare hands
   and laying them down in a neat pile on the shore

I stand in the waves at Far Rockaway and in the little breakers
   at Jones Beach and haunt the Russian restaurants and
   tearooms beneath the el in Brighton and swear to myself
   but I'm only a virgin in the shade of a tree on a blanket
   with my parents

Tactics of evasion give rise to purity of experience

In many cases the petting is limited to simple kisses and caresses

I failed as a child and later with my lover I reached out for

We exist reciprocally in relation to ourselves and to one another,
   but if you go too far away you might cry out "Mother,
   I'm lost" and return to where you began, start again
   with a new person

You might think this book contains everything I know, but
   when you come to the end you say: he's never been
   in love

To have the bodies of one's closest relations eaten by someone
   else is not as good as eating them oneself

It's the light around the edges of the city not the innermost
    self which speaks of trial and error in the judicial sense
    where people are sent up the creek for so many years we
    can no longer recognize them when we see them on the
    street, alive and free

Sometimes he loses the thread of a thought and begins to mumble
    to himself regardless of whether he's talking to someone
    or he's alone, but we don't interrupt him: maybe he's
    talking about us?

He deports himself as if he had tenure, but he can be fired
    at a moment's notice

Guy in sauna says, "Give me a cigarette and a drink. What's all
    this health shit anyway?"

Mummified deity come unbound: a struggle with loss is your
    next obsession

Love isn't a person or thing or an abstract noun meaning
    itself or its derivatives nor is it a person replacing
    an object which you might desire to sleep with, nor is
    it inanimate, this person, nor can it speak, this
    thing, nor can it return love, this harbinger, nor
    stand on a pedestal, this star

And if we had but time to waste, to get wasted, I'd tell you
    the story: I'd call you long distance

We can hum along with the song until the promise of pleasure
    relates to a pronoun which in turn takes the form of a
    person who isn't here

What you say about hell may be a fiction, but she still isn't here

Each step of the day is a dwelling place for memories that
   underline—some might say "amplify"—your present state,
   by enfolding it in rigorous ambivalence of who you've
   become, leaving no stone unturned to the light of day,
   no moment sacred, while establishing a link of certainty
   to the transience of the hours of solitude where thinking
   "goes on" invisibly as an experience of what remains, the
   imminent floundering about of everything, the fin of
   a fish in the ship's wake

You can say of omnipotence a psychiatrist's sanity was
   well-earned

My great-grandfather spent most of his time in a synagogue on
   Pike Street

If poetry arises from some hiding place then I want to sit down
   and talk with that moral eunuch who envisioned the poem as
   a medium between the heart and the brain

An acre of refinement that glows around the border like the
   winning number in a drawing: there are no matching
   socks

I need your attention to appease my anger

People wet their beds when they sleep in a new place for
   the first time

Ideas attached to words look frail in comparison as if someone
   were suffering from the catarrh that was going around

I fastened on a vocation before I knew who I was (my
   identity is a function of my relations with others, not
   what I do)

She rings the downstairs buzzer—I let her in

Moths blew in through the holes in the screen and a sick child
   stirred in her sleep, this was pleasure

On Xmas Eve I hitched over Mt. Tam on the back of a motorcycle

In his lexicon, the word "bourgeoisie" is an object of fear

Leaning your chin on your hand can cause acne—if your hand
   is dirty

My father went into the hallway and began calling for the police
   to save him from my mother whom he didn't recognize
   and whom he thought wanted to murder him and steal his
   money

Ask someone for advice and he says "all she needs is affection"

She was so surprised to meet him she didn't notice he wasn't
   wearing his pants

It's time I look out the window, you pass this way, you say
   you came a long way for nothing: sticker affixed to
   appliance

He limits his experience to what he reads, but content intrudes:
   the radio, the heat coming up through the pipes, the words
   of a song

I can't read the blackboard but I'm too vain to wear glasses

The winds of the gods blow their words in my face

I want to go to a restaurant where the waiters call me "comrade"

There's no risk if you know the results of what you do, no inner
    growth in which recourse to action leads to attrition, no
    flower so insular it can't command its own fee

You can open the tomb in my presence and find the eraser

I guess they better recruit some new players to replace the old
    ones who can barely get up the court on defense and tend
    to stand around and watch the trajectory of the ball
    in its arc as it leaves the hands of the opposing players

"Look," you said, at the seagull on the ledge, but when I turned
    it had flown away

You look like someone I used to know, expressing dismay at my
    pregnancy, maybe the weather

BY THE FIRE

I turned the corner and there was
a goat. It had a bell around its neck
to get it where it wanted to go. Sometimes
there was a golden line that froze in the sky, like the
line that ran down the center of the road,
dividing the road in two as it disappeared
under the car. When I wanted to go somewhere
I stuck out my thumb. What are the customs
of this planet anyway? Isn't anyone home?
I forgot the manners and grace of calling in advance
to say "I'm coming over." I entered unannounced,
without knocking, as if no one cared. Everyone's house
was where one sat down and made oneself invisible, until
    someone
recognized you, saw you were there, nodded and said "hello."
I passed through town years ago and then I disappeared
but when I returned you were sitting in the same chair.
The house had a roof, four walls, and some doors
and a lot of trinkets someone had brought up
over the hill from the city. I ate an apple
on a rock at the edge of the shore. It could be
that if I got angry I might go to sleep anywhere
and the next morning someone would find me, assure
me that nothing was wrong. I've never been able
to stay angry at anyone too long. I bought
the cheapest wine and drifted through life in a manner of
    speaking,
watched the words slip like peas off the end of
my knife. Some mornings I woke with a bad taste
in my mouth, as if I'd mistaken the edge of the plate
for some beans. It might be a good idea not to go
anywhere for awhile, stay put for once in your life
and watch the light pass through the tops of the trees.

I was crossing the field when you stopped and took off
your pants. I was standing on a reef looking down
on a roomful of props. It seems possible that
one can feel jaded from too much love, or from turning
yourself inside out till you become the other person,
and she was the sky and the field you were walking through
led to a tent or the basement of a deserted house.
But it was someone else's bedroom where the sun drifted in
through the curtains and I stepped over a puddle and listened to
the dogs bark just to get to where you were. Was I a fool
to leave you, lying in the sun, untended? In the storm,
when the electricity went out, we ate by the light of the hearth.
You never thought I could learn anything and when you spoke
I pretended not to listen but the next time I made it clear
I'd thought it out for myself and that my manner
of knowledge was my own: the way I did things worked
out all right even if I didn't do them right, in the traditional
sense, as if for you there was only one right way
of doing anything, and that was all. You were frightened that my
    friends
were coming to displace you, so you left, but
before that I walked to your house every night.
I bought bread and wine, we ate by the fire.
It seemed like you had gone to bed before
me and then I was there, but that there were
no more tears or anger or recriminations and that our pasts
had dissolved at last like some huge stalagmite
on the wall of a cave. It was Plato's cave, and the
light at the entrance was like a sprig of juniper
around your eyes. I heard you coming but I didn't know
whether it was you or the horse in the pasture outside
the house. It wasn't your house; you were renting it
from someone else. I came along around five every night.
I climbed the hill with groceries: did I call you
before I came? You were often in the kitchen making
dinner when I arrived. We drank some wine and ate

in front of the fire. I don't think
anyone visited us there, in our house. It
lasted awhile: me waiting, walking up the hill
with the food. I liked the way the trees looked and I was
in love with the past, with someone else, and you tried to steer
me closer to the present with your love for
me that was like all the fireflies and the leaves
of the eucalyptus trees that shadowed the road
as I walked through the door. Occasionally someone
I know stopped their car and drove me halfway. I remember
the place where the road turned and I had to step over
some old logs. It was worth it to see the light in the window
and drink the wine. You were there in the kitchen, I wiped
the rain from my glasses, we embraced. Sometimes the
wires went down and we built a fire, we made dinner on the fire.
You taught me how to build a fire but thought I wasn't
listening. It was like reading *The Odyssey* by
candlelight, it was like travelling through the desert
to a wisp of smoke that was like an oasis of peacefulness not
a mirage of fear and sleep, not a deathmask but all the wishes
of childhood in the warmth of a blanket and a soft bed.
These feelings could extend from me to you and go on forever
as long as memory winds around the edge of the horizon
like a trail leading from town to town. I can be
myself, at last, and say we share this like a parcel
of land, divided in two, no fences: that's where we are.
I brought some wine and some bread and watched as you twisted
the corkscrew into the bottle and pulled the cork free, and
poured the drinks. Was it raining outside? I can't remember,
but it's like a dream to forget the awning of trees
and the lights in the distance where you kneel by the fire
    with the kindling,
brown hair shining on the edge of a star.

BLACK BREAD WITH RUSSIAN DRESSING

Cosmonaut, turn your antiquated gaze
to heaven, know no greater love
when the heart's awake

the gods originate in original sin
one of a kind objects
and novelty items

made to order shirts with
centipedes stitched on the collars, hats
with brims to hide the eyes

like visors. Whenever I see her
I look the other way, she
crosses the street

when she sees me coming. Once
we were people who knew the special
way people feel when they meet

under complicated circumstances.
You might interpret the same event
differently. Water condenses

under room temperature, like poetry.
The caress of a hand still animated
by the thrill of discovery

without yet being blunted by desire
is only a memory.
Were we fixated forever

at that stage or did we change?
The high point of the visit was steak in an all-night diner,
a midwestern variety, she was leaving the next day.

Bite the delicate fingers
that feed you, and portray
it all in bas relief

on the side of a cup, alongside
the astronomical observations
so far ahead of their time

blueprints of buildings
with fake facades
and corbeled arches.

MISTAKEN IDENTITY

There's a little fear piercing
the air at the boundary of the self

it's the same self I saw under the awning
back in '63

Yesterday we saw the mushroom with
the orange flecks that grew up
out of the earth after last week's big
rain

It seems like anyone could shoot an arrow
and pierce my heart

Of love, bursting into flame, I inhale
the sweet smoke, hidden under the pale
refrain of all the old leaves

and now some leaves are falling
around the steps of the porch

and the wizened fish under the dock
are suffering
in our absence

AVENUE OF ESCAPE

She pretends that she's kissing him but their lips never meet

The cop stopped us outside Albuquerque and we dropped our
   dope on the side of the road

I had a way of hinting at what I was feeling without coming out
   and saying it

My sister teaches me to dance the lindy

Many separations end in reconciliation, although many of
   these reconciliations will later give way to new
   separations

The guy who replaced him had no prior experience but was
   willing to work for less than minimum wage

I had an alibi for where I was on the night of August 28, 1985
   but the police still subpoenaed me to give testimony at
   a closed hearing

We hire someone else, a third party, to do our dirty work

When I was thirteen I got up on a stage in a house of God
   (so-called) and sang a song without meaning the meaning of
   which was in the inflections of the words

A 2-ton trailer truck overturned on the Belt Parkway causing
   a tie-up on the Gowanus Expressway

I sing the emphasis of sound to convey meaning to somebody

I go to the store to buy some scallions

The obsession with undoing the processes of the past, the past
    actions and thought, until they're null and void

Once I was a hysteric, now I'm an obsessive-compulsive

Tchaikovsky's 2nd Piano Concerto on the radio: I'm too lazy
    to turn the dial

I shared a hotel room in Barcelona with a guy I met on the train
    who washed his underwear in the sink while I slept

She was wearing flat shoes, a white turtleneck, and over the
    knee socks

They found out the results of the test: positive, positive, positive

It might be sad to note that there are instances when words
    correspond to reality, like the word "reality' when you
    speak it, and the clouds pass in front of the sun

We wanted to go to the movies but I couldn't find a parking
    space so we rented a movie at the video store and went
    home and watched it

All the roaches in the drawer are pregnant

The ancient cutting off the branch of the forget-me-not
    grows to fruition

You can sleep on the couch if you don't want to go home alone

The girl said she saw the murder from the window of her
    apartment, but no one believed her because of her history
    of drug abuse

Nothing I do can make her happy

The restaurant turned me away because I wasn't wearing a jacket
and tie

It wasn't as if I could tell what she was thinking, or wanted
to, but it was like the sun had vanished behind a cloud,
all the light faded from her eyes, and I didn't have to ask
"What are you thinking?" or "What's wrong?," I could
tell what was on her mind by the way she crossed her
legs and tilted her head

The people who spoke out against his policy were confined to
their cells

Three to five with time off for good behavior, twenty-five
to life with no possibility of parole

Out the window, in a moving vehicle, thinking and reading

I may be old, but I'm still desirable

She told me she was pregnant, that I was the father, but that
she was marrying someone else

The distance between stars can be measured in feet and inches

The prison warden's wife runs off with an ex-con

He smiled, and every tooth seemed to have a new meaning

There's no future in becoming something if you can't accept who
you are in the present and realize that the person you're
in the process of becoming is a close relation to the
person you are now

The therapist adjusts her skirt over her knees

She was 8, he was 14, they met in the basement, she touched
 his penis

It doesn't take a genius to realize that combining strong
 analgesics with liquor in great quantities can bring
 hidden personality traits to the surface

He sat in a corner waiting for someone to notice him

The elevator to the lobby was filled with young doctors

I strain my neck staring at the ceiling of the Vatican

You can say I felt helpless, dependent, like a young child
 who just bit his tongue, but when someone paged for a
 doctor on the intercom I snapped to attention

No one suffering from minor trauma, no one climbing the walls

The Latin teacher accuses me of cheating on the final exam

I could tell what she was thinking by the way she looked at me
 as if I wasn't there

It wasn't my nature to depend on my family for salvation but
 if I ever became desperate I would wire them for some
 money

You can pay me back, without interest, a little at a time

The whole class was punished because one student was cheating

The guy at the next table raises his beer bottle in my direction:
 "Hey Bro!"

"I don't think I want to win anything, I want to die unadorned"

The fighter in orange trunks shrugs his robe onto the carpet

It's no longer appropriate to mention our names in the same
breath

An announcement for a tag sale tacked to the trunk of a tree

I remove her denim skirt, her basketball sneakers, her golf cap

Hold back real feelings so they exist in new form complicated by
not "exposing" them to reaction of someone who
hates you

The matinee was no longer during the day, but after hours when
even the quietest street turned its back on tranquility

It's not just because we're human that we want to experience
everything

Once they sat in a theater, alone in their heads

I say things out of nowhere to draw attention to myself,
otherwise I am nowhere

You can let love die without anyone knowing it

There's a half-hour delay at the Lincoln and Holland Tunnels

The man at the entrance to the alley glanced over his shoulder
as he buttoned his pants

MAYBE YOU CAN DEFINE LOVE IN TERMS OF WHAT IT ISN'T

and get back to me—
I have a call on the
other line.

*

The rays of light contain you like
something you might see that exists, but
who can remember the sins I committed
as a kid—did I call them that
innately or was it just a trick to
make me think more about what I wanted,
was that the sin? Describe a paradigm
in which nothing ever repeats itself,
a love you might consider an achievement
or an act of will. You didn't let it die
but stayed true to your own idea of
constancy no matter what anyone else thought
about what you did. Sometimes my actions
belie what I feel, isn't that human?
It's not a sin to step outside yourself
and find something pleasurable about the
light and air, but a sin to deny yourself
pleasure, any shape or form, as it comes
your way. The end
of the story congeals before it begins.
Textures of paint (if the walls could speak etc.)
ruminate on some silence, something said.

*

I'm locked in the bathroom at the party at Bill Berkson's
mother's apartment. Keep turning knob but the door is stuck
    Finally,
I begin banging on the door and calling out for help, until a
woman I'd been introduced to earlier comes to my rescue. "I
thought it was a ghost," she says. We lean back against the sink,
with its gold faucets, and kiss.

*

    The precedent to what I did
    doesn't exist in history (cf Michelet)
    but a kiss is more ignoble than the tomes
    of antiquity, a kiss is not entered
    into haphazardly but with eyes wide open

*

    a helicopter just flew over
    the lake like a brushstroke
    and the same sun I saw yesterday
    disappeared behind a tree,
    the sun's light seems less
    intense this year, don't you think?
    the wind just blew the pink
    inner tube beneath the dock,
    one remains justly yours, now and forever,
    but the kiss is like statuary, blown
    to pieces by the storm

*

"I've lost the will to be prodigious"
one might say, or just "I've
lost it"

*

The unattainable. Falling in love with someone who's already
"attached." A woman you see one day on the beach. Aspiring to
the unattainable in poetry (and in love too).

*

in the afterglow of something
passing like a bird through the
treetops there's the sound
of hammering I heard yesterday and
the days vanish and with them this
thin wafer of desire pressed
under the tongue in all its
purity dissolves in its entirety
leaving a bad taste, a grown-up taste,
a refinement of every taste
I've ever known, something "mature" as
some people might say though maturity's
just a form of reticence in its way,
a state of decay

I took LSD for the first time at Liam O'Gallagher's loft in San Francisco. After a few hours I decided I wanted to be alone, hopped the cable car up California Street to my apartment on Nob Hill. Back home, I "thought" I'd come down and figured I should probably eat something—it had been a while. I made myself a steak and some frozen vegetables and sat down at the small table looking out at the garden. When I realized I couldn't lift my knife and fork in the proper manner it occurred to me that the drug had changed me in a permanent way, that I'd never be the same person again. Not only wouldn't I ever eat again, but I wouldn't write poetry either.

*

There must be incentives
other than acquisitiveness and fear
that make us want to do one thing
more than another

*

"We met by the Xerox machine," David, a bond trader, relates. "She'd just been hired, and I was enthralled. I can't put my finger on anything she said or did, but I was certain, certain, that she felt the way I did. We were chatting about God knows what, nobody else was around, and I said to myself, 'I'm going to do it this time. I'm going to grab her right here, run my hands down her, kiss her until our teeth turn to powder.' And then I thought,

'Holy God, what if I'm wrong? What if she starts screaming?' So I just stood there on the edge like that, chatting pleasantly, like a pitiful helpless giant."

*

we're kidding ourselves if we think
we can accomplish everything
in the time that's allotted us
let's do all we can without putting
off till tomorrow and in general
prevaricating about everything the way
we did in the past when time
had that feeling of infinite longing
like looking into the eyes of a cat
or dog and realizing this animal isn't
looking at you but at something you can't
see that's beyond you (infinite space and air)

*

it might happen that you would
consider someone else's feelings, and
in that way learn something
you didn't already know

*

It's Washington's birthday. Beverly takes Marie to "Amadeus." I take Max to Washington Square Park. Bernadette stays at home (to work on the dollhouse) with Sophia. Blue sky through the branches and the flag waving in the breeze.

*

"Does this mean that whatever exists does, in some sense, contain you?"

"Is the whole of creation too small to hold God?"

overlapping—"is the same part of you present in all things at once?"

"Who can recall the sins I committed as a baby?"

"grown-up games are known as business"

"Every soul who sins brings its own punishment upon itself"

*

should we state our needs
clearly or keep them secret
like the bird
we know
desires warmth and attention
but what if it learned the meaning
of words like "desire" and "want"
would we allow its
feelings to take precedent

over our own
or would we remark to ourselves   imagine
as we often do, about people
what it would be like
to be a bird   see
the world through

                                        her eyes

                          *

To be alone with oneself
is beautiful, and that indigenous phrase

like all human contact ripening on the stem
and the voice inside still speaking for everyone.

Latching on to something and then holding back
as if frightened I'd gone too far, only it wasn't

my own soul I was looking into
but something even more vulnerable, here

are her eyes in which I can see myself
and the vortex of a calm reflection

which isn't perfidious or the opposite
of whatever that might be, sublime?

                          *

one rails against the impertinence
of others, in the impersonal sense,
talking about poetry instead of sex

*

I take Sophia to see "Amadeus" (Sunday afternoon). On the way home we stop in Washington Square Park where I meet Bruce and his daughter. He's completely gray but still handsome. I know he's been in jail but we don't talk about it. Instead, we discuss apartments, real estate, different neighborhoods—how they're changing and where we might want to live. I tell him that my landlord offered me $20,000 to move. He tells me I should take the money and buy a building and rent it out. "You have to become a bit of a capitalist, Lewis."

*

Is love these two people
locked in a haphazard embrace? Or
is some more feasible entity
created that insists something beautiful
must occur, pertaining to bliss,
and the desire to give—is that what it
means?

*

Says Toni, a senior vice president with a major cosmetics firm, whose affair with a colleague almost destroyed her career: "There was a time when women just didn't do any buying. The men traveled in packs, and their wives had the normal fear of one-night stands. Then, when a lot of women were promoted to that level, the wives would say, 'You're not going on a trip with her. What do you mean, you're going for four days to Florida with so-

and-so!' The man would say, 'Don't be silly, it's business. I'm a professional, this is my job!' Well, that's nonsense. They may set out on business, but the temptations are enormous. You don't have to worry any more about how you're going to stay out for the evening and explain it to the spouse. I mean, you're totally free! You're in a motel, you're having drinks, and this young handsome guy whom you've just been talking to is in the room next to yours, and what the hell, you're in Kookamonga!"

*

it's your own opinion
I want to hear
not what others think
to convince you because
they talk louder, act
more aggressive
don't go home and worry
it's your passive self
that relinquished hold
on your ideals
in the face of a tirade
at the edge of the balustrade
hiding under an umbrella
like a subsidiary organization
whose heart is present
in name only

*

Mohammed tells me he works at a bakery from 7 to 5, then goes to classes every night. He's trying to save money to bring his family here from Nigeria. He apologizes for sometimes falling asleep during my class.

*

Only the simple things matter now: making breakfast for the kids, taking them to school, reading them books and playing scrabble and bingo.

*

From now on nothing's going to seem real except the simple things like washing dishes and cooking dinner.

*

(coda)

I see some comprehension in life's sorrows, but
I turn away from the dark
for a while I forgot my work—I had other things to do
jobs to earn money to eat and pay rent
I wandered through the world with dignity, saying
    hello—
and then taking your hand—or goodbye, and grasping
    your shoulder
in a friendly way
all day the rain tossed my boat against the shore
but ecstasy was a mirror
with a narrow frame

I could pass through like a door
arrive at some new place
(neither heavyset nor thin)
Sometimes I'd kiss someone I didn't know
just to show that affection was still possible
and just to see the look of surprise pass over her face
as if to say: Really! I didn't know you cared–

ANYONE BUT YOU

I went to pick berries on the road to paradise

They call themselves Communists but all they want are
   dishwashers and big cars

A light without shadow generates an emotion without reserve

Members of the staff leave the institution after an 8-hour shift,
   but the inmates stay forever

He can ask someone for money without losing his self-respect

My mother didn't know what I wanted for my birthday, so she
   gave me some money

I put my money on Awe Inspiring but it came in last

Border violations between genres were reported by the authorities

Type poems on stencils, run them off on the mimeo machine, call
   up friends to help collate and staple, mail copies into
   the world

I have some knowledge of her but maybe I'm thinking of
   someone else

I think of what I'd say, what I could possibly say, if we ever
   met

The place becomes the words you use to describe it but your
   feelings about the place have a life of their own

At parties we went to the bedroom where the guests stashed
their coats, locked the door, swept the coats onto the
floor, and took off our clothes

I changed my religion to please her parents, but they still
hated me

New words are needed to heal the rift

We avoid each other in the bookstore, we pretend we don't see
each other, I think you must feel guilty for not answering
my last letter, you don't realize how much I love you,
your last book was great

There's a beach all for yourself with a sign that reads "No
Trespassing" tacked to a tree

How fortunate we are to be separate from the sea at last
(mer = sea, mère = mother)

Mansions where executives once lived with their families will
be split into apartments for the families of the workers

The cab driver orders me out of his vehicle: I owe him 17 cents

I postpone pleasure so I can enjoy it more later, boredom of
expectancy when no one comes

We go to her house and sit on the living room sofa while her
parents sleep inside e.g. maybe tonight she'll let me put
my hand inside her blouse

The desire for objectivity harbors the intrusion of jealousy

It seems like you might never stop loving her, and then you do

There's the movie theater where I saw "Rocco & His Brothers"
(dubbed version), there's the schoolyard where I played
"asses up"

In the fairy tale, a wedge of cheese falls from his beak into
a puddle

We can't tell the players on the scorecards without sleeping
with them

Last year at this time, or ten years ago, or twenty, a quarter
century passes by as if it were a quarter hour, or a minute

When I was nine I hit a girl on the shoulder with a stone to
get her attention

This house will never be empty of the torment of loving

We heard on the news that Deng Xiaoping had died, but it was
only a rumor

"No sweat" one might say as the solution to anything

I took a special speech class in college because of my lisp

Madonna's "Like A Prayer" on radio in schoolyard: it's the first
day of summer

We smoke a last cigarette together before changing the sheets

I can spend in 5 hours what it takes me 3 days to earn

The used car salesman told me that he had a Buick with 130,000
miles on it for $1,600 that ran like a dream

I was in bed with her, in a dream, and her husband came in and
said: I'm going to shoot you

I return home even though I know she's in bed with someone else

I opened the door with my key but she had put the chain on
before she went to bed

Five Cubans calling for the ouster of Castro handcuffed
themselves to a railing inside the crown of The Statue
of Liberty

You return home on a crowded subway late at night full of
resentment

Employers not only refuse to take on employees past the age
of 35 but hesitate to put their confidence in someone who
has never been "permanently employed"

You light a thin cigarette and then put it out after taking
one puff

You go out for a container of milk and slam the door behind you,
you curse under your breath as you take out the garbage

The Story of O tells of love as well, but in a different light

I was standing on a platform in the 14th Street subway station
when a guy pointed a gun at me and another guy pressed
a gun against the side of my head and said to my
girlfriend: "What's a chick like you doing with this
faggot"

The people in the cars wave at me as I walk across the bridge

I see myself crossing the bridge, I'm going back the way I came

It's too late for me, but maybe you can learn from my experience

She knew I was coming home some day, but she didn't know
exactly when

There was a chain on the door but she didn't hear me when I
called her name

You can't call him a "bachelor" or a "sadist" and expect me
to know what he's like

The blue of the Gitanes pack on the table in the stranger's
apartment

Back in the village, in the presence of their weeping sisters,
the Marines were humiliated by their instructors

I look up words in the Thesaurus to make my poems sound more
interesting

He was fired on Tuesday, without notice, and we never saw him
again

Saw an apartment on 13th Street, between 1st and A, three small
rooms for $800, but didn't take it

PICTURES

Something the tenses reveal
as they return to themselves
a hole to be filled
with perfect thoughts
a rent in the fabric
where repression rests
a patch over the place
where the rent appears
not a hole but a wedge
of which I can only say

that once I loved
the light on the hillside
across the lake
and once I heard the cars going by
on the Panhandle
and once I listened to her step
on the stair
and once I lunched in my chair, alone,
while the fan droned on.

THE FLEA MARKET IN KIEL

1

Miracles of incidental longing
fill in the blanks. The same
words all over again but in different
colors. A kiss on the mouth
goes a long way. The person
behind the cactus plant lowers
her eyes.

The pablum runs down the sides
of her face. It's an honest face
with windows where
the soul is visible. It would be
importune of me to walk up
to her and ask her to dance.
My chest contracts at the thought.
Fake tears get in the way.

They claimed that the source
of his stomach problem was something
he ate. Like shellfish? I wanted to say
but held my tongue.

Even your best friends won't tell you.
The fine print tells us nothing
we don't already know. A floral bouquet
for someone no one remembers.

A rock carved by Michelangelo
in the form of a snake.

2

It speaks to me in a voice
forever clear. The clarity
is the uncertainty
like a dead skunk on the
side of the road. Lost
highway where no
one says what they
mean. Not the
troubadours, but people
living on the edge. Mountain
people encamped in a cave
in the foothills. An escapee from
your past who lights up the
page. A gong show reject.
Your boyfriend?

3

This dream is no longer in service.

A fake house, a blue facade.

Anonymous voices whispering behind
the bedroom wall.

The animals gather at the fence
to eat from my hands.

The one who stands out and the other
who blends in.

The muse of innocence and decrepitude intertwined.

4

I wear special goggles
to keep the sparks from
blinding me. I cross the street
when I see you coming.
Please define your terms:

"depressed" "persevere" "opprobrium"

The higher I go the darker
it gets. The authorities
turn me back at the border.
They stare at my passport
and shake their heads.

Desire will come
when least expected.
Desire will come like an
inflammation of the jaw.

February: the sunset.
No tenants meeting
in lobby. A hailstorm
at midnight. To the child
a dog?

5

Let it be said, in the aftermath of everything, that I was wandering
in a kind of bardo and that I returned to life, with my body
intact and my breath uncertain, and that you, who I thought
had been missing in action, was standing beside me, as always,
to point out the way.

6

I'm sorry you don't understand the rent is due
every month. If you don't pay the rent the landlord
gets angry. How angry depends on who it is. He might hire
someone to let the air out of your tires or post a summons
on your door. I'm afraid you're going to have to hire
a tenants rights lawyer.

The dog under the table
eats the scraps from my plate. The coral is the color
of sunlight on water. All I can hear is the sound of my
breathing underwater. My breath is audible only to myself.
There are stones embedded in the surface of the reef.
The surface of the reef is covered with small stones.

7

She has to be home early
so she can make dinner for
her brothers. The cloud of
unknowing, a luxury liner
off the southern coast.
Cemeteries that resemble whole
cities but are even more orderly.
A time of internal growth
where every breath counts
for something.
Let's escape what was given
going in circles the same
words. A rosary, the catechism,
an amber barrette.

8

My dental insurance doesn't cover my family.
But today I found out I can borrow on my retirement plan.
My heart is still beating, but I don't know for whom.
For an encore, I'll sing "Some Enchanted Evening"
or "Up on the Roof."

9

I like the way the world folds back on itself like a hinge.
I feel a terminal disappointment, as if you had forgotten my
name on the letter and it came back unread. All the
gravel under my feet leading up to the driveway, and the house
in the distance, the ampersand between house & feet, the
slate-covered roof angling over the flowerbed. I want to come
in from the rain, through the backdoor, up the steps where
the grownups are getting drunk and removing the screens
from the windows. Before night comes, I'll repair to the corner
store for a 9-volt battery and a bag of litter. They say "the night
is young" but when you're gone it lasts forever.

10

You can say "Restoration" and then you can say
"drama." And then you can see there's a hill to
climb backwards.

You have to get your ass
in gear because the boss wants you to do something.
The assignment is due next week: better check
for spelling.

There are no ashtrays so put out your smoke
in the palm of your hand.

The last night on earth wasn't all it was
cracked up to be. You don't know it's going
to be the last night when it's happening. If it
was really the last night you'd do something
different. (Why is this night different from
all others?)

"When you left me," the song goes, but
I know the next line. It seeps out of the grooves
into someone else's heart.

Now that I have responsibilities I'm going to
turn my life around. This could mean
a drop in blood sugar. Did you take
your shots?

The music is coming
from an upstairs window. It
might be Handel
but it could be Verdi.

11

Perhaps rain falls like holy water
in the forest

but you didn't hear it

the wings of the eagle, or something
less prurient

something that snaps in two
when you breathe on it, *mi dispiace*

the lost state of bliss

the redeemed and the irredeemable

all you need are a few sentences
to paraphrase

what you didn't hear—a back draft
of eternal mindfulness

directed at no one

12

There is no one to kiss.

We go through a tunnel and the window blackens.

Smoke pours from the roof of some tiny cottage
in the middle of nowhere.

Boring romanticism rears its head

and smashes the butler over the head
with a pair of tongs. I close my book

and stare straight ahead.

I want to kiss you
I think, but don't.

13

One of them throws a ball
in the air when no one's looking.
My Polish landlady is watering

her flowers. It was fresh
in my mind but I interrupted
myself nonetheless. "I have
to think it over," I said to no one.
You can't drink from the bottle
without removing the cork. I've
seen the deadness in a person's
eyes in which the language of
feeling was lost, to whom the
permission to feel anything had
never been granted. There was
never a day like this one when
the sky unfolds and the boat
on the edge of the horizon disappears
from view. We close our eyes
in disbelief, lost in the mist on top
of a mountain with the gods. Isn't
anyone home? The sign was written
in a kind of primitive script. I sat
on an embankment staring
at my plate of alligator steak.
The juice in my glass was red.
It was almost summer.

14

And then Diana Ross and The Supremes were singing "Stop! In
  the Name of Blub"

But as I was leaving the theater I realized I could no longer
  understand the words

Because of all the people in the audience who were singing along

Or possibly we can say it was a faulty sound system

Or more to the point maybe all the words began to blur in my
    head

The way people look alike when you see them from a distance

So the words and the sounds never convey the same meaning

Or when I thought they meant something it was really the
    opposite

The glitter in Diana Ross's hair, for instance, or her dress
    which consisted

Of thousands of tiny sequins (blinding, really, as she tottered onto
    the stage)

Each sequin a tiny mirror reflecting the sun, the stars and the
    planets

That make up a galaxy where existence is a bad dream

From which you wake up in a cold sweat, hair matted
    to the sides of your face

The indentation of your head on the pillow—

Diana, shut up.

15

Once I was a jealous husband walking down Avenue B.
And once I boarded a plane and flew to Athens.
Once I hitch-hiked on the back of a motorcycle over a mountain
    on Xmas eve.
And once I coughed and woke you up in my sleep.

I want to steal away, into the darkness, where no one else has
    gone.
The cold sun harbors loss at the foot of my chair.
A man with a cue card appears in the wings and everyone weeps.
It occurs to me that my audience consists of no one but you.

16

Now I will know myself
in the broadening vision of things that have already
happened, and steal away past the abandoned
factories until the river melts like burning cotton on
the other side of the road, and all the buildings
of brick and tenement slide into the gully
across the bridge.

Let it be known that the bridge was built by people
you don't know, that "all things flow" to the surface
on the edge of the sky, holding it in place
like the stars hold your face in a container
of happenstance without consequence
or desire.

17 *for Katt*

Not the pumping
of air
in and out
of the lungs

eating
lest the body
fall asleep
sleeping at night

from weariness
of the flesh
Life Soul Life
I have felt it

with you
you
the light
and you

the genial warmth
that has made
the closed germ within me
to expand

and you
the sweet influence
that is to cherish
its perfect flower

ACKNOWLEDGMENTS

Thanks to Sam Truitt, George Quasha, and Susan Quasha at Station Hill, and to Michael Ruby for initiating this project, close reading, and overall support.

Thanks to the editors and publishers of the books where these poems first appeared: Bill Thomas (Toad Press), Joe Brainard (Boke Press), Anne Waldman (Angel Hair Books), Ted and Joan Wilentz (Corinth Books), Andrew Crozier (Ferry Press), Larry Fagin (Adventures In Poetry), Alan Davies (Other Books), David Rosenberg (Coach House Press), Lita Hornick (Kulchur Press), Bernadette Mayer (United Artists Books), George and Chris Tysh (In Camera), Barbara Henning (Long News), Donald Ellis (Creative Arts Book Company), Patrick Masterson (A Rest Books), and Steve Clay (Granary Books).

Also thanks to Joanne Kyger, Bill Berkson, Tom Clark, Mushka Kochan, William Corbett, Lee Harwood, Gloria Frym, Douglas Messerli, Wang Ping, Daniel Kane, Lisa Jarnot, Bill Kushner, Kyle Schlesinger, and Jed Birmingham. And to cover artists Pamela Lawton, Louise Hamlin, Rackstraw Downes, Joe Brainard, Rosemary Mayer, Donna Dennis, Yvonne Jacquette, George Schneeman, Emilie Clark, Martha Rockwell, and Alan Saret.

Special thanks to Marie Warsh, Sophia Warsh, Max Warsh, Alyssa Gorelick, and Zola Ray Warsh.

Photograph by Max Warsh

Lewis Warsh is the author of over thirty volumes of poetry, fiction and autobiography, including *Alien Abduction* (Ugly Duckling Presse, 2015), *One Foot Out the Door: Collected Stories* (Spuyten Duyvil, 2014), *A Place in the Sun* (Spuyten Duyvil, 2010) and *Inseparable* (Granary Books, 2008). He was co-founder, with Bernadette Mayer, of United Artists Magazine and Books, and co-editor, with Anne Waldman, of *The Angel Hair Anthology* (Granary Books, 2001). He has received grants and awards from the National Endowment for the Arts, the New York State Council of the Arts, *The American Poetry Review* and The Fund for Poetry. *Mimeo Mimeo #7* (2012) was devoted to his poetry, fiction and collages, and to a bibliography of his work as a writer and publisher. He has taught at Naropa University, The Poetry Project, Bowery Poetry, SUNY Albany and Long Island University (Brooklyn), where he was founding director of the MFA program in creative writing (2007-2013) and where he currently teaches. His new novel, *Delusions of Being Observed*, was serialized in The Brooklyn Rail beginning October 2016. (www.lewiswarsh.com)

CPSIA information can be obtained
at www.ICGtesting.com
Printed in the USA
FSOW01n0520291217
42492FS